# RECLAIMING
# JOY

Your 4-Step Guide to Happy, Healthy & Free

*May the words on these Pages nourish and inspire ya to Be who you are - Joy! Enjoy! Stephanie :)*

## STEPHANIE FILARDI

Reclaiming JOY: Your 4-Step Guide to Happy, Healthy & Free

Published and distributed in the Unites States by Stephanie Filardi . To contact the publisher, visit

www.thrivingyouthrivinglife.com

ISBN-13: 978-0692663639
ISBN-10: 0692663630
Library of Congress Control Number: 2016904404

Printed in the United States of America

*"Perhaps they are not stars in the sky, but rather openings where our loved ones shine down to let us know they are happy."*

This one is for you, Dad.

*Lokah Samastah Sukhino Bhavantu*

*May all beings everywhere be happy and free, and may my life, in the way I choose to glorify it, contribute to the health, happiness, well-being, and freedom of all.*

# Acknowledgments

To all of you who have courageously lived your life according to who you are, moving to your own drumbeat, I honor you and thank you from the bottom of my heart. You have deeply inspired my being, and this writing.

To my mentors, colleagues, clients, and friends who have encouraged and supported me in speaking my voice, many blessings to you.

Writing this book has felt at times both terrifying and exhilarating, like a birthing process. I am humbled by the experience. I want to give special thanks to my power team of love and support:

Christine Filardi, thank you for always reminding me that "Yes, I can" and for being exactly who you are by living the life of *your* dreams.

Peter Iocovello, deep gratitude for your authentic partnership and unconditional love over the years since I've known you. You are a beacon of light. I am forever humbled and in awe of your ability to love deep and laugh out loud. Namaste.

To my family at Bronxville Wellness Sanctuary, I love you, I love you, I love you! Thank you for your dedication to improving the well-being of others daily by sharing your gifts. Your beautiful faces and generous support have forever filled my heart and touched my soul.

Mom, thank you for allowing me to be me, even when it didn't make sense. It's the ultimate gift.

Jill Mason, my Shakti sister and incredible editor, deep gratitude for your expertise and love in birthing this book.

And finally, to David, my love, thank you for showing me what real commitment looks and feels like. You are a blessing.

# Contents

Introduction ...................................................... 1

JOY Replies ...................................................... 3

**Chapter One: Finding Your Joy**...................... 7

**Joy – What Is It?** ............................................8
Awareness and Right Questions ........................8
✳ Reflection Exercise: Define Joy ...........................14

**Foundations for Joy** .................................... 15
Health – Energy, Stress, Food ........................16
Relationships – Self and Others ........................19
Career – Being and Doing ........................22
Life Purpose – What and Why? ........................ 24
✳ Reflection Exercise: Foundations for Well-Being ...........25

**Is Joy a Choice?** ........................................ 26
Path, Practice, and Fruit ........................26
✳ Reflection Exercise: Joy As Choice ...........................28

**Chapter Summary and Reflection**...................... 29

**Chapter Two: Powering Up for Joy** ................ 31

**Darkness and What It Reveals** ........................ 32
Meet Your Shadow........................32
✳ Reflection Exercise: Hello, Shadow ...........................37

**Transforming Darkness into Light** ........................ 38
Fear and Acceptance ........................38
✳ Reflection Exercise: Love and Light ...........................43

**Lessons of Light** ............................................... **44**

Meaning, Forgiveness, Healing, Empowerment ...................44

✳ Reflection Exercise: Forgiveness Letter....................51

**Chapter Summary and Reflection** ...................... **51**

# Chapter Three: Following Your Joy ............... 53

**Grounding**........................................................ **54**

Relaxed Mind, Balanced Emotions...........................................54

✳ Breathing Exercise: Nadi Shodhana Pranayama..............58

**Getting There**.................................................. **59**

Visualization, Action............................................................59

✳ Visualization Exercise: Use Your Imagination ...............63

**Inspired Action** .............................................. **64**

Inner Alignment............................................................64

✳ Reflection Exercise: Check Your Alignment ....................66

**Chapter Summary and Reflection**........................... **67**

# Chapter Four: Living As Joy............................ 69

**Know Yourself**................................................. **70**

Scheduling, Spaciousness, Saying NO .................................70

✳ Reflection Exercise: Know Where You Are .....................77

**Commitment and Discipline**............................. **78**

The 3 Big Excuses: Not Enough Time, Money, Knowledge ...78

Excuse #1 – Not Enough Time.....................................................79

Excuse #2 – Not Enough Money..................................................82

Excuse #3 – Not Enough Knowledge ...........................................90

✳ Reflection Exercise: What's My Excuse? .......................91

Sweet Surrender ........................................................ 92

En-joy and In-joy ........................................................92

❋ Reflection Exercise: Experiment in Surrender ..................98

Chapter Summary and Reflection...................................... 99

Resources ........................................................ 101

Speaker Highlight ........................................ 105

x

# Introduction

*"The privilege of a lifetime is being who you are."*

—Joseph Campbell

My story is about reclaiming joy. You see, joy is *who we are*. It's at the core of each and every one of us. Don't believe me? Keep reading. If you are like me, at some point along your journey, your joy got buried or lost. Perhaps it was claimed by a sudden traumatic event you experienced. Or maybe your joy was slowly claimed by your experience of being alive in a world that can be painful.

However it happens, at some point, if we're lucky, we wake up to the reality that we are not, in fact, happy. The things we thought and were taught would bring us joy don't. Once this reality sets in, one of two things might happen. One is that you become depressed, disconnected, and drained. You get so tired and stressed that you give up. You make the choice to live out your days joy-less. To survive, you tell yourself things such as, "This is life," "Others have it worse," "I should be happy I'm alive." And yet you feel anything but alive! This may cause you to engage in behaviors that put you further away from joy.

Or you may feel that something is wrong with you, or that there is some wisdom you are missing! Maybe you read books (like this one!), take classes or work with a professional to help you find out exactly why you aren't experiencing joy.

Wherever you stand (I've experienced both), I am joyfully here to tell you that your days of joyless living can come to an end. *If you choose to reclaim joy, this book is for you.*

My story is about how I spent the first chapter of my life living by the principle of driving myself really hard. I was driving to do and

1

accomplish. I was driving to control. Ultimately, I was driving to be someone I was not. This was exhausting and not sustainable.

I believe our bodies don't lie. While we may push ourselves into driving hard, at some point the body says STOP. Often, the body actually does stop, or at least gets our attention. For me, this moment came the day I felt in my own chest what I knew my father had experienced as a heart attack three years earlier. He didn't survive. I was determined to.

Here's what happened. At the time, I'd been driving myself hard in all areas of my life, from career to relationships, and it was taking a toll physically, mentally, and emotionally. I was working for a retail startup company, and on that day I was preparing to open a new store. Before I got on the road, I was checking my email. There it was – the email that sent me right over the edge. The details of the message aren't important. What is important is that in that moment, I felt the heart attack coming. My physical body was no longer willing to play that hard-driving, joyless game. The tension I felt in my chest got my attention big time. In that very same moment, I heard my father's voice plead, "Stephanie, I didn't raise you this way, run for your life." That day, I gave my notice to my employer and have not looked back. In that moment, I decided I would no longer abuse myself or take abuse from others. *The time had come for me to stop driving and start thriving.* I made a commitment to myself and embarked on a journey that would ultimately support me living happy, healthy, and free. I made the choice to reclaim joy.

In the chapters of this book, I will share with you the step-by-step process of how I have put into practice reclaiming joy. My heart's desire is that by sharing my experiences here, you will gain insight into your *own* life and see how you may begin reclaiming joy. Perhaps some or even all of this book will resonate with you. But if I simply inspire you to consider the *possibility* of reclaiming joy in your one precious life, I will have accomplished my goal. As for me, my vision is a big one! I imagine a world where joy is our barometer for living. Will you join me?

# JOY Replies

While writing this book, I decided to ask a range of people how they defined joy. My heart bloomed wide open with gratitude and joy for the replies I received. Below are some of my favorites:

*"JOY is one's elated heart and internal peace which emanates when one is fully present – in THIS very moment in time; not merely dwelling in the regrets of one's past nor the projected worries of the future "*

—Mark Armiento, LMFT, CASAC

*Joy? I define joy as a "decision." By deciding to be happy, to love, to find joy in everything I do and to be grateful for what & who I have, it helps me to set boundaries and to be truly joyful in my life. It's a decision I must make every day.*

—Luchy Camacho

*Journey*

*Of*

*Yourself*

*I find joy in each step towards self-discovery.*

—Nazaré Rodrigues

*Joy is waking up every morning and loving Life to fullest, but the real joy is being aware of how good life can be.*

—Barbara Reveron

*Joy is being at peace with oneself, unfettered with life's attachments, complications, demands, and toxic people.*

—Phyllis Toohey


*Joy is what I feel when I look at my cats basking in the morning sun, or looking into the eyes of someone I love, the innocence of a child or a beautiful sunset.*

—Patty Meehan, Yoga Instructor


*For me, joy is the feeling of being truly known and accepted by another human being to whom I can offer the same in return.*

—Michele Bogin


*Joy is when you can't stop smiling!*

—Daria Kelty


*Joy is the ability to be present, completely present, with exactly what is. Real joy comes from the acceptance of EVERYTHING and knowing that life does not need us to improve it or make it better, but to experience it fully and relish in ALL the sufferings and joys it has to offer.*

—Devarshi Steven Hartman


*JOY for me is family, friends, fun, and a glass of wine.*

—Eileen S

*Joy is when my heart is open wide and welcoming all the wonders the world has to offer to me. Joy is when I get an idea that is so thrilling and excites me so much that I want to grab my boobies!*

—Amethyst Wyldfyre works!


*Joy is laughing out loud at myself every time I am blessed to see my inauthentic self. Joy is laughter.*

—Maati Sanovia


*For me, joy is a feeling of simultaneously being at ease with the past, feeling peace in the present moment, and embracing hope for a blessed future.*

—Adrianna Melnyk


*JOY: being freed of the constraints of what others think. Living life by your standards . . . what ultimately speaks to you.*

—Chris Canning


*Joy is being me. . . . And the beauty that comes from total acceptance as I walk, run, fly, and stumble my way through this journey.*

—Anita Ancel, Shaman Coach


*Dinosaurs.*

—Deborah Skilliter

Reclaiming Joy

## CHAPTER ONE
# Finding Your Joy

*"It is better to perform one's own duties imperfectly than to master the duties of another. By fulfilling the obligations he is born with, a person never comes to grief."*

—The Bhagavad Gita

## Reclaiming Joy

Congratulations! You have taken the first step to reclaiming joy. By first step I mean of becoming aware that something is perhaps missing from your life or in need of your attention. In this chapter we will begin to raise our awareness of the concept of joy by exploring three questions:

What is joy exactly?

What is joy for you?

Is joy a choice?

Fasten your seatbelts my friends. We are going on a journey!

# Joy – What Is It?

### Awareness and Right Questions

I am amazed at how often in life we are not happy simply because we lack awareness. I would even go so far as to say that one of the main reasons we are not happy is because we have not (yet!) taken the time to ask, "What is joy?" The excellent news is that if this is true for you, *now* is the time to choose another way. The process of reclaiming joy starts with awareness and ends with choice.

Take a moment to consider this: Is living joyfully a choice? What I have learned over the years is, yes, it most certainly is. I will discuss this in more detail later in this chapter. For now, suffice it to say that in life all of us experience things we perhaps would not choose. Yet when faced with the more difficult of life's curve balls – death, divorce, and illness, to name a few – *we do have a choice* as to how we will live in the wake of these experiences. In fact, it is often in the most difficult times that we are forced to wake up and begin asking questions. I have learned that questions create the foundation for awareness and pave the way for choice, when we are willing to see it that way. In my life, losing my father was a most powerful lesson in this.

When my father died of a sudden heart attack in 2004, three weeks before I was to be married, it quickly woke me up. I realized there were two choices I had to make. Both choices led me to where I am today. The first choice I had to make was an immediate one: Do we still have the wedding? The second choice came a bit later.

As to the wedding, we chose to proceed with everything as planned. At the time, it felt like the right decision. Keep in mind that this was during my hard-driving days. I was the strong one. I didn't need help. I wouldn't allow myself to break down. The show had to go on. On top of that, I felt a sense of responsibility for keeping my family together. Eventually, that behavior would take a toll. From the time my father passed until I got divorced several years later, there were many times when grief stole my joy. One time in particular stands out – I recall walking down the church aisle during our wedding ceremony unable to lift my chin. I had tears in my eyes. I remember feeling so *conflicted*. I felt as if I *should* be happy because it was my wedding day, but all I felt was sadness and loss. As I would learn later, much of my conflict came from not *allowing* myself to break down and to feel all of it. This too would take its toll. After all, there is only so much we are able to push down before we either implode or explode.

The second choice I had to make was about my own health and well-being. Losing my father so unexpectedly was a serious wake-up call on many levels. My father wasn't overweight, didn't drink or smoke, and exercised daily. He seemed content enough in life. How did this happen? What I would later learn was that he was under a lot of stress, the chronic kind. By chronic I mean constant. It's the kind of stress that feels like there is no end in sight, and it's a silent killer.

When the body is under chronic stress, the stress hormones adrenaline and cortisol are dumped into our bloodstream. This is useful and necessary for our survival in times of "fight or flight," as in the days when we hunted for our own food. When these hormones are released, our heart and breath rates increase, our senses become sharper, and we have more energy and strength to fight off our predators. Unfortunately, today many of us live continuously in this fight-or-flight mode. Our modern-day predators may be anything from never-ending to-do lists to concerns over job security. Over time, the effects of these stress hormones take a toll on our body. They include muscle tension, headaches, digestive issues, anxiety, depression, inability to concentrate and memory loss, and heart disease. In her *Washington Times* article "Chronic Stress: The Silent Killer If Not Managed," Dr. Nina Radcliff writes, "In fact, the American Medical Association states that chronic stress has put us 'in the midst of the worst degenerative crisis in the history of humankind.'"

I believe chronic stress is what took my father's life. His heart simply couldn't take it anymore, and his physical body stopped. The way I see it is that my father dying was the ultimate sacrifice he made for me. While his physical death set him free from the physical, emotional, and mental pain of being such a tender soul, it also set me free. It set me free to make choices about how I would carry on in the aftermath. *Would I use this an opportunity to awaken and begin to live the life of my dreams, or would I bury my head in the sand?* I chose to begin living my dreams. As I will share with you, it hasn't been a direct, easy path! It has been curvy, wild, and at times excruciatingly painful and difficult. Yet everything I have encountered has been in service to reclaiming joy in my life. By learning how to do that, I am humbly able to share this with you.

At the time my father died, I felt stress in all four foundational areas of my life: *health, relationship, career, and life purpose.* I was ten to fifteen pounds overweight and eating my fair share of fatty and sugary foods. I was drinking too much alcohol and had a tendency to drink in order to "relax." I was conflicted about my career. I was between corporate jobs and unsure that I was cut out for the rat race I was used to. I longed to work in a field where I could make a positive difference in people's well-being, yet I had no idea how that could happen. As for my romantic relationship, it was hard for me to be present. As I said, I was experiencing a lot of conflict. I was holding the loss and grief from losing my dad alongside the idea that I should be happily building my own family. I was lost. I was scared. Food, alcohol, shopping, working, and being busy all the time became my "medicine." I was self-medicating to avoid the pain and the grief that lurked within. I was filling the void I felt. I was in life, yet I didn't feel ALIVE.

In addition to feeling conflicted, not present, and somewhat dead inside, I felt even more responsible for taking care of everything and everyone. After all, I was known as the "doer." Looking back, I realize that being the doer made me feel in control. If I was in control, I felt safe. As I continued to drive myself harder and harder with all the doing, naturally, my stress mounted. I was living in the exhausting vicious cycle that endless doing creates.

I drove myself hard at work, unable to disconnect even when I wasn't working. Since I prided myself on being busy all the time, if I wasn't working, I was exercising. I drove myself hard at the gym, as well, often working out with trainers until ten o'clock at night. I valued getting things done and wasn't happy unless every moment was booked. I was on the hamster wheel, fueled by those stress hormones I spoke of earlier.

I was *doing* all these things I thought would and should make me happy, but I wasn't happy. I was doing to avoid feeling. I was doing to fill the void. What I would later realize is that "doing" does not bring joy. Doing, however, will push our limits so much that ultimately we are forced, as I was, to stop. When I finally did stop, I was forced to face myself. It was intense, and it was when my "inner work" really began.

As traumatic experience often does, my father's sudden death forced me to look at something very precious – the reality of time. I realized we have no guarantees as to how long we have here in the flesh. It occurred to me that I could choose to drive myself hard in life to feel accomplished and have a nice "retirement," but what if I didn't make it to retirement? What if I worked myself so hard, I ended up sick and unable to enjoy the fruits of my labor? Or worse, what if I died young? When I turned thirty, I began to believe I wouldn't make it past forty. Suddenly, it no longer made sense for me to live in the future. I had to start living in the present moment and paying attention to my health and well-being. Things had to change. If I didn't want to end up like my dad, I would have to start making different choices. With this new awareness, I was faced with the life-altering questions of what do I do, and where do I start?

As often happens when we truly commit to change, the universe helped me. I was introduced to Stephen R. Covey's book *The 7 Habits of Highly Effective People*. My kind of title, for sure! Being a doer, I love being effective. For those unfamiliar with his book, essentially it outlines how to take control of your life by making changes based on sound principles. What struck me most while reading it was his emphasis on looking at life holistically and affecting change from that vantage point. For example, instead of living a life centered on some combination of money, career, family, pleasure, and even church, he advocates centering your life on principles. What is the reasoning behind this? He states, "As a person fluctuates from one center to another, the resulting relativism is like roller coasting through life". Basically the up-and-down effect that this fluctuation creates leaves us devoid of consistent direction, wisdom, and ultimately the energy necessary to forge ahead. Instead, Covey says, "By centering our lives on timeless unchanging principles, we create a fundamental paradigm of effective living. It is the center that puts all other centers in perspective".

Covey's ideas made so much sense to me. I realized the choice was mine to make about what principles would guide me going forward. The enormity of this realization was at once frightening and quite thrilling. Until that time, perhaps like you, I had been more or less reacting to life. Armed with fear and curiosity, I felt I was onto something much deeper, yet I had no idea what. What I did know was that I wanted to do as Covey said and design my life around principles I felt would support my well-being. The principles I chose were awareness, peace, and joy. It was at this time that I turned to meditation for support. I'm so happy I did.

Meditation became a most powerful awareness practice for me, and my life began to change. The more I practiced meditation, the more I noticed behaviors that truly didn't support my happiness and well-being. Slowly I began to choose meditation over self-medicating. In doing that, I started to understand the power of nonjudgmental compassionate self-awareness. It became clear that my life would start to shift in a positive direction when my actions were rooted in awareness, self-love, and compassion. With that in mind I began to pay far more attention to *how I was being* rather than *what I was doing*. Then it hit me! Until then I really had no idea what joy meant. Perhaps like many of you, I'd been confusing joy with happiness. But, as I've since discovered, happiness and joy are not the same. *Rather, joy is a state of being.* I would even say joy is *a state of well-being.* Being in a state of joy for me includes feelings of peace, equanimity, gratitude, love, awareness, groundedness, presence. Yes! These were the principles I wanted to design my life around.

You see, when our state of being is one of joy, we are able to experience the full range of human emotion. We will still experience sadness, loneliness, and anger, but we won't get stuck in those feelings for months, years, or even a lifetime. Instead, because our foundation is joy, we are able to ride the waves of emotions. When being grounded and present become our guiding principles, we are able to *witness* the emotions running through us rather than overly *identifying* with them and therefore becoming them. We understand that emotions come and go.

When I previously defined joy simply as happiness, I was seeking something fleeting. Happiness comes and goes with the ebb and flow of life. By chasing happiness, the door was always open for me to feel depressed about something. Then the desire to self-medicate to fill the void would invariably arise. But staying committed to my meditation practice helped me ride the waves of emotion and shed light on how I was *being*. Through meditation I learned how to stay grounded and present in order to embrace joy as a state of being. By choosing joy, I began to experience life in a much more peaceful way. With joy as my foundation, sadness and loneliness don't scare me as they used to. I allow the feelings to come and go because I know that at my core I am joy.

Embracing joy led to another lightning bolt: What was I really reclaiming? *By reclaiming joy, what I was really reclaiming was my true self. I began to understand that being joy is being ME!* Wowsers. Sounds so simple, doesn't it? Yet for many of us being who we are is one of life's biggest challenges. As I began to study this concept of being oneself, I turned to books written by Joseph Campbell, a writer and lecturer on the topics of mythology, religion, and the experience of being human. He is noted for the phrase "Follow your bliss." I became enamored with his work, and eventually his quote "The privilege of a lifetime is being who you are" became the overall *guiding principle* on my path to reclaiming joy.

As I will share in the pages that follow, *the journey to reclaiming joy is a personal journey for each of us that comes down to being who you are, not who other people want, expect, or need you to be.* The process of reclaiming joy is about understanding what does and does *not* support your well-being, and then choosing what does, with apologies to nobody.

The truth is, the choice to reclaim joy, is an invitation for us to dig deeper into who we are and who we are meant to be. As Joseph Campbell so beautifully said, "We must be willing to let go of the life we planned so as to have the life that is waiting for us." Indeed. How do we start this process? We start by asking questions. It starts with awareness, my friends!

### ✳ Reflection Exercise: Define Joy

Take a few minutes and write your response to the following question:

How do you define joy?

_____

_____

_____

_____

_____

_____

_____

_____

_____

_____

## Foundations for Joy

When I embarked on the journey to reclaim joy, I looked at four key areas of my life that I felt were *foundational* to my personal well-being: health, relationships, career, and life purpose. I believed that if I understood how to feed and nourish these four areas, on a continual basis, not only would it enhance my well-being, it would also support me in being who I am.

During this time another book, *The Right Questions* by Debbie Ford, entered my life. It helped me to understand how I got to where I was based on the choices I had been making. Ford lays out ten profound questions designed to inspire and empower you to *consciously* create the life you desire, one choice at a time. As I looked at the four foundational areas of my life, I kept returning to one question in particular: "Will this choice propel me toward an inspiring future, or will it keep me stuck in the past?" By asking the "right" questions – or "quality" questions, as I like to call them – we put ourselves in a position to make quality choices.

As we go along, how we define well-being in the foundational areas of our life may shift over time as a natural result of our growing awareness. In the foundational area of relationships, for example, although my divorce was a dark time in my life, it was ultimately for my well-being. I didn't get married thinking it would end in divorce, of course. And yet my divorce forced my eyes open and gave me an opportunity to dig deep into the unhealthy self-medicating behaviors I was using to avoid being present for myself and my life.

Throughout this process of reclaiming joy, if we stay fully engaged, we will grow. What we may define as supportive of our well-being in our foundational areas at one time will likely change as we gain the courage and clarity to live more fully into who we are. We may even add or delete foundational areas entirely. At this stage of the process my invitation to you is to practice beginner's mind. Stay open to possibility. Perhaps what is waiting for you is *much bigger and better* than you could ever imagine. Believe it!

# Reclaiming Joy

## Health – Energy, Stress, Food

The first area foundational to my well-being is health. Health incorporates many things, as it relates to our physical, mental, and spiritual selves. When I began asking quality questions about my health, I focused on *three areas*: energy levels, stress levels, and food. I considered health on a spectrum. On one end of the spectrum of health there is "sick." On the other end is "optimal" health. In the middle of the spectrum is "unsick." As I looked around, it seemed that many people, myself included, were in the "unsick" category.

For example, many of us go through the day using sugar and caffeine to stay awake. Why do we do this? Survival! We are sleep deprived because of the thoughts that keep us up and the never-ending to-do lists. Some of us drink too much alcohol because we are stressed and depressed. Others eat too many processed foods because we are too busy or tired to cook or even care. This combination leads to low energy, weight issues, and a weak immune system. We catch the same cold everyone else does. When we are sick, we go to the doctor for medicine to feel better. While we do get better with medicine, the cycle continues; we are unable to experience optimal health. We remain in the "unsick" category, often too tired to go out and enjoy life, even when we get time off. Is this how we are meant to live? No way! It seems more like surviving than thriving – and, my friends, we are born to thrive.

So, after my father's death, I was determined to achieve optimal health. For me, this means having the necessary energy to live the life I desire. When I started to examine what affected my energy levels, adequate sleep was at the top of the list. The more I read about sleep, the more I learned that our bodies heal and recover during sleep. Sleep is "vitamin R" – rest – and without enough of it, nothing works well for me. Realizing this, I consciously began making sleep a priority, getting at least eight hours each night. To help me fall asleep, in addition to my daily meditation practice, I decided to stop watching and reading disturbing things one hour before bed. Ultimately, I gave up watching the news and reading the newspaper altogether, which has greatly improved my overall energy and outlook! The stimulation and negativity that are often presented result in a useless energy leak that I want no part of.

Let's face it, when we are tired, it's hard to have patience and think clearly. When we add the stress of daily living on top of being tired, it's no wonder we turn to unhealthy and excessive behaviors such as unhealthy or overeating and excessive drinking, shopping, or working, to name a few. As I started getting more sleep, I noticed my improved energy levels, better food choices, and an ability to manage my stress in healthier ways. I made exercise and meditation a priority. As I did that, I naturally wanted to eat better. I became mindful of what, and perhaps more important, *why* I was eating. In the process I noticed unhealthy patterns of emotional eating. I had been using food to deal with stress and to fill the void. I began to ask myself, "What are you really hungry for?" *I was using food in an attempt to fill the emptiness I felt from denying myself the privilege to be myself.* As you may imagine, the unhealthy eating patterns had led to difficulty managing my weight. I was heavier than I wanted to be and felt uncomfortable in my body. I wanted to be leaner, lighter, and healthier overall.

I began using my meditation practice as a way to become more mindful of my relationship with food. I wanted to be a healthy weight, and I was determined to do the necessary work to make it happen. In the past when I wanted to lose weight, I tried all the different diets. I ended up feeling a sense of deprivation, and the weight always came back. This time I was no longer willing to go on a diet or count calories. Deep down I knew that if I began listening to my body and cultivating a healthy and respectful relationship with food, the weight would come off naturally. That's what happened.

I began to ask quality questions such as "Am I hungry, or am I simply feeding my stress, exhaustion, or emptiness?" I didn't always like the answers, but I stayed on the path, and another miracle happened! I was introduced to the book *Women, Food and God* by Geneen Roth. Her book forever changed my relationship with food. She says, "When you no longer believe that eating will save your life when you feel exhausted or overwhelmed or lonely, you will stop. You will stop turning to food when you start understanding in your body, not just your mind, that there is something better than turning to food. And this time, when you lose weight, you will keep it off. Awareness, not deprivation, informs what you eat. Presence, not shame, changes how you see yourself and what you rely on".

She was talking my language big time. Awareness. Presence. Yes! I felt the journey to healthy weight was not only doable, it was sustainable. Finally, I gave myself permission to deeply listen to what my body was hungry for. Food? Love? Rest? Connection? When I ate, I noticed how I felt afterward. Did my food choices support my desire to feel energized and healthy? Did I feel satisfied? Powerful quality questions.

As I began to bring mindful eating into my life, I also began to enjoy food much more. Once used to self-medicate, it now became a healthy means of deep nourishment for me. I learned how to cook easy and healthy meals and loved sharing them with others. The act of cooking and sharing fed me on many levels. Even when I wasn't able to cook, I was (and still am) excited to discover healthy "to-go" and restaurant options. Luckily, restaurants and food stores were beginning to get the message on the healthy and tasty food front. For me, cultivating a healthy relationship with food (and later with alcohol) enabled me to reach and maintain a healthy weight.

Today I experience high energy levels and minimal stress. I am in love with my body. I feel strong and healthy. Taken together these things form the foundation of health for me and allow me to enjoy my life. I make choices that support the priority I place on being healthy. Having said that, of course I allow myself leeway every now and then. I call it my "85/15" rule. Eighty-five percent of the time I have discipline, and fifteen percent of the time I indulge. When I do indulge, it isn't to excess. I no longer crave or need the excess. If I am out to dinner and want a cocktail with my meal and carrot cake for dessert, I order those things. And I fully enjoy them! As a result of cultivating a healthy and respectful relationship with food and alcohol, I am able to enjoy both in moderation, without the guilt.

The same is true for sleep. Do I get eight hours (sometimes ten) every night? No. Yet because I do most of the time, I still feel good and can get through the day without overdoing it with sugar and caffeine when I don't.

The same is true about stress. I am human. There are days when I lose my cool, for sure. However, those days have become fewer and fewer, and the amount of time it takes for me to "relax" is less and less. By now, you may be thinking how simple this sounds on paper and wondering how to actually do it. I'll share more about how later in the book. Keep reading, my friends.

## Relationships – Self and Others

The second foundational area to well-being is relationships. For some of you it may seem obvious that relationships are a major part of what brings us joy. For others, perhaps relationships are exactly what bring you anything but joy! Whatever the case, my intention is for you to come away with a deeper understanding of how both our relationship with our self and our relationships with others have a huge impact on our ability to be who we are and experience joy.

In my experience, the relationship we have with ourselves influences how we treat others and reveals much about where our growth in this area resides. For example, part of my life's work – and it is ongoing — is the practice of nonjudgmental compassionate self-awareness. I am a strong, driven person. I hold myself to high standards and often place high expectations on myself. While this has enabled me to create the life I desire, at times it has also been a challenge. Sometimes I feel that I "fall short" and relapse into judging myself. If I place those same high expectations on others, and they fall short, it's not hard to imagine how I may judge them. The reality is that judging another is painful for *both* people. The person being judged gets upset. And at some point, the one doing the judging ends up feeling pretty lousy! As I have learned to be compassionate with myself, I have learned how to extend compassion to others. The result? Drastically improved personal and professional relationships. It feels better, too.

Another example of how our relationship with ourselves may reflect our relationships with others is how we talk to ourselves – our self-talk. When something doesn't go our way, or we make a mistake, what do we tell ourselves? Do we say *negative* and mean things, or are we *positive* and forgiving? If we're negative toward ourselves, it's more likely we will be negative in dealing with others when a challenge arises. There are many more examples of how our relationship with ourselves is telling of how we treat others. Suffice it to say that all relationships are mirrors of who we are, who we want to be, and even who we *don't* want to be. For me, this realization makes nonjudgmental compassionate self-awareness an ongoing practice – a practice that meditation helps me with. In the next chapter I will reveal more about this.

In my experience, when we understand ourselves, it's easier to cultivate satisfying relationships with others. What I have found is that *conscious* relationships that are positive, supportive, and authentic fuel my joy and support my well-being. Anything less than this builds resentment and takes a toll on my emotional energy. In time, the relationship will adversely affect my physical energy, as well, via lack of sleep and stress. The combination impacts my ability to experience joy and quite frankly doesn't feel good. Do you know what I mean? Let me explain in more detail.

A *positive* relationship is one in which we feel good overall, even energized after an encounter. We genuinely enjoy the people who make us feel that way, and we want to be around them. It doesn't mean things are always peaceful. It does mean that those people take responsibility for their energy and are aware of and care about how they are showing up in the relationship. They genuinely value positivity and look for it. They respect and appreciate people and life itself.

*Supportive* relationships are those in which we feel the other person cares about our well-being. They are attentive to our needs. While they might not always agree with us or understand us, they accept us and allow us the space to explore who we are. They support our desire to be ourselves. And that enables us to return the gift!

An *authentic* relationship is one in which we are able to honestly and openly express how we feel and truly be ourselves. We hide nothing. We feel safe, even if at times we feel uncomfortable and vulnerable. We have tough conversations when necessary and advocate lovingly and openly for what is important to us. We face the truth with courage and grace, and our intention is to help one another be the best person we can be. We allow the relationship to change form, or even end, if that is required for our spiritual growth. In an authentic relationship we realize people aren't being "unkind" to us when we don't get what we want. Rather, we realize that either they or we are simply not in the place we desire. This realization makes it easier to choose joy when the going gets tough. Authentic relationships provide a fertile ground for us to mature, gain wisdom, and fully be ourselves.

There is one final thought I'd like to share about relationships. While I was going through my divorce, I had the blessing of reading *Coming Apart* by Daphne Rose Kingma. Her wisdom helped me understand why my marriage ended and how I contributed to that. It softened the pain and gave me hope. Her book also revealed to me what I needed to learn if I truly wanted to be in a conscious relationship that supported my well-being and enabled me to be who I am. *I realized that in order to have a positive, supportive, and authentic relationship, I needed to be that person first.* By being that person, I would eventually attract another such person. Kingma says, "It is the creation of the self – living exactly and wholly as ourselves possibly can – that is our primary task as human beings. Because relationships assist us in accomplishing this purpose, I see their endings not as tragic, but although needled with pain, as potent opportunities". After reading her book, I understood that being in a conscious relationship is a necessary ingredient in reclaiming joy. Why? Conscious relationships give us the space to be who we are . . . joy!

# Reclaiming Joy

## Career – Being and Doing

The third area foundational to well-being is career. Many of us spend most of our waking hours at work, and so I feel it is important to understand the *role* our career plays in reclaiming joy. In studying this, I asked myself, does our job have to be our passion in order to live joyfully? What I've come up with is that the answer depends on who you are. For some of us, having a career that's aligned with our passion is essential for joy. For others, it's not. It is a *very individual* matter. In my experience, whether we experience joy around our career depends more on our *perspective* and who we are *being* in our world of work than on whether we are working in our "passion." As I will share, even when we are doing something that we are passionate about, we may not be experiencing joy.

Let's start with those of us, myself included, who feel it is essential to have a career that aligns with our passion. When I left the corporate world, I made a decision to pursue work in which I could make a positive difference in people's well-being. Initially, my work then was in the wellness field, doing nutritional and holistic health coaching. At the time, I felt that if I was engaging in work I was passionate about, making a positive difference in the lives of others, I would *automatically* experience joy. Boy, was I wrong! Even though I was pursuing work I was passionate about, I wasn't experiencing joy. I eventually learned that I was still pursuing something intangible.

While working with clients on nutrition and holistic health, once again I saw how food was a powerful doorway to our interior world. Not only was I being asked to help clients work through food issues at a deeper level, I was being called to look at my own life in a deeper way, as well. The question became Why aren't I experiencing joy even though my career is aligned with my passion?

Eventually, this question, and my desire for deepened awareness, led me to pursue training in yoga, meditation, and shamanic energy healing. The funny thing is that while my ego said I was doing all these trainings

22

for my clients, I later realized that I was *also* doing it for myself. It wasn't until I began to dig deeper into how I was *being* in relationship to what I was *doing* that I was able to uncover why I was unable to experience joy. When I came to terms with the truth that I was doing what I was passionate about yet was not able to experience joy, it was paralyzing.

Appearing to have it all together sometimes enables us to get away with a lot. In my case, I knew my stuff and was sought after for my knowledge. I was very well versed in nutrition and recognized as a source of inspiration. My clients saw results. Yet inside I still felt a void, an emptiness. I had a sense of searching that seemed endless. How many more certifications would I need until I feel joy? It became exhausting. Ultimately, it was not sustainable. I knew it, and I felt it.

As my fortieth birthday approached – yes, I made it to forty – I began to feel tightening in my body in the area of my chest. My physical body was once again giving me the warning signal to STOP. Like the first time, I stopped and paid attention. The fear I felt gave me the courage to make one of the best decisions ever. I chose to take a time out, a six-month sabbatical. What happened as a result of my sabbatical is the reason I am writing this book, at this time. I will share more about this later in the book. What I will say here is that my inability to experience joy was a result of being focused on the wrong things. My perspective was twisted, and it affected how I was being in the world. What I was doing didn't matter. I could have been doing my dream job. What mattered, which I now understand, is how we are *being* in the *doing*.

How we are *being* in the *doing* is why I feel not all of us need to be in the career of our passion to experience joy. It seems to me that some people are simply grateful to work, to earn a decent living, and that is enough to bring them joy. Others choose work that provides a significant income to support a lifestyle of material pleasures, and that brings them joy. It doesn't matter. There is no judgment here. We all have different desires, and that is part of what makes life so rich. The point I am trying to make is that career isn't everything. Career is part of the foundation, and whether we experience joy is more about how we are being in our work than about what we are doing. Over time, as our doing and our being align, we may transition into a career that is more deeply connected with our spirit. As this happens, we may begin to ask the question Why am I here, anyway? This question, asked throughout the ages, is another part of the foundation for joy.

### Life Purpose – What and Why?

The fourth area foundational to well-being is life purpose. Some of you might be thinking, "Life purpose" – what do you mean? Perhaps you have not ever considered this question. Others of you might be at the other end of the spectrum. You are so identified with your life purpose that it informs everything you do. It doesn't matter where you are on the spectrum, but how life purpose relates to our ability to experience joy is something you will want to consider if you have gotten this far in the book.

In my experience, to live joyfully we need to understand what this experience of being human is all about. Meaning, *why are we here*? What is our role, and what unique gifts do we have to offer? Understanding this, and then embodying it, brings us beyond our limited self, our ego, and connects us to life.

When we are choosing joy as the path, the answer to the question of why we are here will reveal itself. If we are not able to find a sufficient reason for our being, then we will be disconnected from who we are, and it will be hard to experience joy. We may spend our life in the endless cycle of doing and searching without ever experiencing the sheer bliss of simply *being*.

Knowing my life purpose grounds me. It gives me direction. It takes me beyond my limited (ego) self. My life purpose connects me to people, places, and experience – to LIFE – in a way that I wouldn't otherwise know. Here's the really cool part: Whether our life purpose is "right" or "wrong" doesn't matter. What matters is that in moments of struggle – when we feel lost, scared, or contracted and question everything and wonder What is the point of this sometimes painful human existence, our life purpose can bring us back to our true, higher, divine self. My life purpose is inspired by the Sanskrit mantra "Lokah Samastah Sukhino Bhavantu." The translation I use to guide my life is "May all beings everywhere be happy and free, and may my life, in the way I choose to glorify it, contribute to the health, happiness, well-being, and freedom of all." Frankly, this is what gets me out of bed every day.

Like some of you, I am fortunate to be able to express my life purpose in both my personal and my professional life. Because this is important to me, during my career transition, I examined the question of why I am here in order to connect my work with my life purpose. Another blessing occurred to affirm my path when I was introduced to Stephen Cope's book *The Great Work of Your Life*. He says, "We work first because we have to work. Then because we want to work. Then because we love to work. Then the work simply does us. Difficult at the beginning. Inevitable at the end". That passage takes my breath away every darn time I read it. The work I do in the world is my life purpose.

Finally, connecting to my life purpose is a returning home of sorts that restores my spirit to gratitude and grace. It gives my life meaning. My life purpose is the star that illuminates my path when at first it seems there is only darkness. My life purpose draws me forward. It helps me get out of my own way. It expands me, opens me to possibility, and enables me to choose again and again to reclaim joy. Understanding my life purpose supports my choice to live as joy, because my life purpose is *who* I am and *why* I am here!

### ❋ Reflection Exercise: Foundations for Well-Being

Take a few minutes to list the foundational areas of your life that are important to your well-being. Do any areas need attention?

---

---

---

---

---

# Is Joy a Choice?

## Path, Practice, and Fruit

Now that I've shared with you that joy is a state of well-being, do you think joy is a choice? I say yes! Joy is a choice. Why do I say this? Let's face it. There are many situations in life – death, loss, illness, to name a few – that may cause us to suffer. Human nature is such that it is easy to fall into the victim role and believe the world is a bad, scary place when bad things happen to us or to those we love. In my experience, in order to live as joy, we must first consciously choose joy as a guiding principle for our life. Once we do, we position ourselves on the path to making it happen.

Let me explain.

Most of us have had the experience of dealing with a challenging love relationship at some point in our life. Whether it was with a lover, parent, sibling, or friend, at some point we have felt betrayed, misunderstood, not seen or heard or loved or some combination. Perhaps the relationship endured but continued to be a challenge. Maybe the relationship ended altogether. Regardless of what happened, there was heartache and instances when it made logical sense to allow the ending of the relationship to steal our joy. Even if everything else in our life was good – a job we enjoyed, good health, and so on – we might allow this one area to completely take over. After all, matters of the heart are deep. But when we live our life based on principles, we are able to gain the perspective required to support our well-being and live the life we desire. We are able to stand back and view the situation less emotionally, and we realize that we get to choose. The question becomes will we allow heartache, or whatever else, to steal our joy? Or will we see heartache for what it is? It's part of being human. In this way we are able to choose a different action. Perhaps instead of falling into the role of victim, we could choose to burn our pain and use it as fuel for our journey. Empowering, isn't it?

I decided to burn my pain. I decided to make joy *the path*. By path, I mean a guiding principle for my life. That principle allows me to be aware of what does and does not bring me joy based on whether a thing supports my well-being and allows me to be myself. For example, eating healthy food brings me joy. Eating junk food does not. With this awareness, I am able to make decisions that support my needs and in turn support joyful living. What's amazing, especially as it relates to food, is that it's no longer about "having the willpower" to eat healthy. It's not a battle. I simply have no desire to eat junk food. Did it happen overnight? No! It's a practice. At first, it required discipline and diligence. Over time it has become a way of life.

The decision to make joy my path revealed to me that I also had to cultivate joy *as a practice*. Anything in life we want to "be good at" we practice. We make it a priority. We commit. The same is true of joy. In order to live as joy, to fully be ourselves and honor our needs, requires practice. This is where we have our work cut out for us, my friends. More will be revealed in the chapters that follow. For now, consider that when we truly commit to making joy a practice, the universe will test us.

It's true! When we commit to joy as a practice, we will be put in situations that test our ability to *stay in joy*. If we stay on the path, it will reveal to us the places we are stuck or blocked. Practicing joy one hundred percent of the time, not only when things are going well, or when we feel like it, but also when things are tough gives us the most amazing opportunity for deep self-discovery, healing, and transformation. In Michael Singer's book *The Untethered Soul*, he says that we are only ever in one of three stages: heading into a crisis, in a crisis, or exiting a crisis. Wow! Yes, another game-changing realization. If that is the case, we will have many chances to *practice* joy. What's incredible about choosing joy as the path and the practice is that ultimately, joy is the fruit, as well!

When we commit to making joy the guiding principle of our life, and we take the practice seriously, we will end up experiencing joy – *the fruit*! Our efforts pay off. We will reap the reward. *We will be free to be who we are.* Easy? Not at first. Worth it? Absolutely! If you don't believe me, try it for yourself.

Think about a situation where you feel anything but joy. Then choose joy as your path. Meaning, if joy is your guiding principle, what do you have to do – how do you have to be – in order to shift your perspective to one of joy about the experience? Next, commit to joy as an ongoing practice. Remember that when you commit to joy as a practice, the universe will reveal to you what is blocking you from experiencing it. Are you being judgmental? Controlling? Fearful? What needs to shift in your own perspective and then your behavior to help you truly embrace joy as a practice?

As you reclaim joy by choosing it as the path and the practice over and over again, you will experience joy as the fruit. Therefore, joy becomes the path, the practice, and the fruit. Simple! We don't have to focus on anything else. We only have to focus on being joy, which boils down to being who we are. Still doubtful? That's okay. The mind will *doubt* and rightfully so. The mind longs to know "how." That is the job of the mind. It is up to us to be aware enough to doubt the doubt. Fear not, my friends. We will satisfy the mind with "how" in the pages that follow. For now it's important to know where you stand on the question of whether joy is a choice. In my experience, if you believe, as I do, that joy *is* a choice, you'll be more likely to embrace the "how," otherwise known as the work or the action of reclaiming joy.

## ✳ Reflection Exercise: Joy As Choice

Take a few minutes to answer the following questions:

Do you believe joy is a choice? If no, why not? If yes, what gets in your way of experiencing it?

_____

_____

_____

_____

_____

_____

_____

_____

## Chapter Summary and Reflection

In this chapter I asked what joy is and encouraged you to reflect upon how you define joy. I spoke about what I consider the four foundational areas of life – health, relationships, career, and life purpose – that contribute to well-being. You may want to add or subtract from these when thinking about the foundational areas of your life. The chapter ended with the question "Is joy a choice?" I believe joy is a choice. By now perhaps you have a better idea of what joy means to you or are at least considering the question. Maybe you are also starting to notice the foundational areas of your life that need attention and realize the power of your choices to support you in reclaiming joy. Well done. As I mentioned, knowing what nourishes us starts with awareness and asking questions.

In the chapter that follows I will discuss what gets in the way of experiencing joy. As we wake up to the life we desire, and choose to live as joy, we also have to face and work through the obstacles that stand in the way. In the process, we learn and use that wisdom to empower ourselves on our journey to being joy.

Before moving on, take a moment to check in with yourself. How are you feeling about these ideas? Excited? Scared? Confused? Angry? Perhaps some combination of all these emotions? If so, great! You are in a very special place. This is the place of awareness. You are waking up. Contrary to popular belief, the process of waking up isn't all sweet and lovely, filled with chocolate and roses. The process of waking up is at times deeply emotional, unsettling, and scary. So pause. Exhale. You are alive! And I have more amazing news for you. *You* get to choose what *you* are willing to do.

*"We can decide to be happy, to give joy before waiting to receive it. This is not denial, but affirmation of the power inside us. Embracing joy heals depression."*
—Marianne Williamson

## CHAPTER TWO

# Powering Up for Joy

*"Nothing ever goes away until it teaches us what we need to know."*
—Pema Chödrön

Will you use your awakened awareness about what it means to reclaim joy as an opportunity to wake up more fully to the life that is waiting for you? If your answer is yes, which I trust it is, I invite you to use this chapter as an opportunity to find even more clarity about what gets in the way of you reclaiming joy. On the pages that follow you will learn how to reclaim your power in support of your journey to reclaim joy. Keep in mind that faith is believing in what you don't (yet) see. Have faith in yourself.

## Darkness and What It Reveals

### Meet Your Shadow

Sweet darkness, what lessons do you have for me? No question, on the path to reclaiming joy we will face difficult times. As I mentioned previously, when we commit, the universe wants to know how serious we are. How strong is our desire? There's a rule the universe operates by without fail, as Paulo Coelho says in *The Alchemist*:

*"When a person really desires something, all the universe conspires to help that person to realize his dream."*

So you see, when we really desire something, and we have the courage to fully commit, *we will be invited to explore whatever it is (good or bad) that stands in the way of getting what we want.* The key is to stay open to what is revealed in the place we often think of as "bad," in the "darkness." I will share how we stay open later. For now, it is important to understand that the darkness is where our gems are hidden. We must befriend the darkness. Unless we make the darkness our ally, we will miss out on the richness of life.

The truth is that many of us miss the opportunity to explore this hidden treasure of gems buried deep within ourselves. Why do we miss it? Because we are terrified. If we face the music, face the truth, what happens then? In addition to being afraid, most of us don't even know where or how to begin this process of exploration and excavation. The walls we have built are so high, and our defenses so strong, we feel paralyzed. What to do? After we have *consciously chosen* to reclaim joy, we need to *lay our defenses down.*

In John Mayer's song "Heartbreak Warfare" there are two lines I simply love. One is "If you want more love, why don't you say so?" Great question! Maybe because we don't *know* what we want. Or perhaps we do know and are terrified to admit it or ask for it based on our past experiences, present beliefs, or future projections. When we commit to the deep work of treasure hunting, our blocks will reveal themselves. As long as we stay open, we will reap the reward.

Similar to making the choice to reclaim joy, and commit to the path, we need to make the choice to stay open, no matter what. The other line I love from John Mayer's song says, "I swear to God we are going to get it right if you lay your weapons down." YES! Lay our weapons down. What? Me? Weapons? Yes. This is the place of being totally open and willing to look at *how and why* we have built walls around us. No question, the walls served us for a time. They kept out the "bad" stuff and kept us safe. The point is, these same walls have also kept out the good stuff. As we reclaim joy, the walls must come down. We must lovingly lay our defenses down. We must be willing to stand naked before ourselves. There is simply no other way.

By now perhaps you are more open to hearing about this place of "darkness." I first learned about this concept, also referred to as the "shadow," while reading *The Shadow Effect* by Debbie Ford. She talks about the shadow as the parts of ourselves we want to deny or disown. They are parts of ourselves we feel shame, regret, or guilt around and, quite naturally, want to repress or resist. Yet, on the contrary, it is by befriending these shadow aspects of ourselves, and bringing them into the light of our awareness, that we have the opportunity to reclaim ourselves. As we do this, we also reclaim our power.

On the path to reclaiming joy, embracing our shadows is essential. When I was ready to face myself and my excessive drinking, I looked at *why* I needed to numb out and relax with alcohol. What I realized was that I didn't feel comfortable *being* who I was. I felt repressed. I was at a point in my life where I wasn't speaking my voice or setting boundaries in personal relationships or at work. It took its toll on me in terms of stress in my body. I longed to have fun and let go. But I was so tightly wound from keeping everything inside, and from driving myself so hard, that alcohol became an easy and quick solution. When I drank, I felt free. When I had a buzz, I felt open, at ease, fun. I enjoyed myself and others so much more! Of course, there was another side to the excessive drinking that showed up afterward, in the days that followed. I felt physically awful – from bad food choices, not enough sleep, my poor liver detoxifying – and emotionally drained from poor decisions I made while under the influence. This added to feelings of shame I already had about my physical body from being overweight as a child (that's another book!). I also felt shame because I didn't know a healthier way to relax, let go, and enjoy, one that didn't involve alcohol. It was hard to admit that I had to drink in order to relax and enjoy.

The interesting paradox about our shadows is that the more we try to repress them, the more energy we give them, and the more they will persist. Until I faced the truth – that I had to drink in order to relax and enjoy – nothing would change. When I faced that truth, it dawned on me that I had been *giving my power away* to alcohol. On some deep level, I incorrectly believed that I *needed* the alcohol to be who I already was and am.

You see, alcohol doesn't change who we are at our core. In his book *Power vs. Force*, David R. Hawkins explains this brilliantly, as follows:

*"The common belief is that it's the substance itself to which the victim has become addicted, due to that substance's power to create a 'high' state of euphoria. . . . Alcohol or drugs do not, in and of themselves, have the power to create a 'high' at all. . . . The actual effect of drugs is merely to suppress the lower energy fields, thereby allowing the user to experience exclusively only the higher ones. It is as though a filter screened out all the lower tones coming from an orchestra so that all that could be heard were*

*the high notes. The suppression of the low notes does not create the high ones; it merely reveals their presence."*

This concept blew me away, and ultimately provided me with the wisdom I needed to change my relationship with alcohol. When I realized that I have the power, not the alcohol, my perspective began to shift. It became clear that I was using alcohol to *suppress* shame, stress, grief (lower tones) in order to feel joy, ease, and peace (high notes). This awareness would not have been revealed to me unless I'd been willing to face and own my shadow parts.

By embracing the parts of myself where I felt shame, I was able to admit that I longed to feel joy – the high notes! I wanted to be able to let go, relax, be myself, and enjoy my life. I had a choice to make, and I made it. I chose to use this experience of darkness to reveal *my* light, *my* high notes. This light, these feelings of joy, ease, and peace had always been there. They were simply being covered up. The walls I had built to keep out the dark, to suppress those lower notes, *also* kept my inner light from shining forth. The walls kept me from experiencing joy, from being who I am. Wow, talk about a lesson of a lifetime! Recounting this to you makes me think of something the Buddha said that I heard during a Bikram yoga class, "One moment can change your day; one day can change your life; one life can change the world." Life is a series of moments strung together. What we make of each moment is our choice.

Following the path to reclaiming joy, and in the process choosing to engage in my own shadow work, has revealed to me what it takes to live in joy, ease, and peace. Quite simply, it takes courage to create peace. For me the courage has come from feeling empowered by two lessons I've learned doing shadow work. The first lesson is that what we resist will persist. The second lesson is that shadow work is a lifelong process.

What do I mean by what we resist persists? Well, it's another law of the universe that conspires on our behalf to support us. While we are in "resisting" mode, it might not seem like the universe is trying to help us. But, if you believe as I do, that the universe is always working for

35

# Reclaiming Joy

our well-being, the persistence becomes a gift. At times the persistence shows up as the little voice of our higher self that is trying so hard to get our attention. Typically, we ignore that! Persistence also shows up when something we think we want to happen doesn't happen. Later, when we look back, we often realize something *even better* happened. Perhaps the most challenging way persistence shows up is when something traumatic happens.

The universe (aka our higher self) will do *whatever* is required to get us to stop, look, and listen – to stop driving and start thriving. So, yes, sometimes the lessons are painful. Sometimes it would be easier if we'd listened to that little voice from the start. But we are human. Being human means that we have a lifetime to *practice* shadow work. Over time, as we lay our defenses down, practice nonresistance, and face our shadow, the process becomes more bearable, if not always fun. Ultimately, if we are committed to the path of being joy, the process becomes part of *who we are* and *how we live*. We integrate shadow work as another awareness practice and have gratitude for the lessons.

This brings me to the second lesson shadow work has taught me – it is a lifelong process. The more we become who we are, meaning the more we make choices to support joy as a way of being, the more our shadows are revealed. Why? Well, if our intention is to be joy, anything that stands in the way will present itself so we can do the work to clear it. Some shadows take many years to be revealed and a lifetime to own. Remember: no judgment. Simply being aware that it is a process and that it is in service to our utmost well-being, which is living as joy, the work becomes worth it. I would even dare to say the work becomes less tiring, and, in some cases, when we get really good, it becomes a form of "sport." I say this because I have had experiences of truly seeing my shadow for *what it is* and *what it wants*.

The truth is, my shadow is an aspect of me, and what it wants is to be seen, loved, and accepted by me. Quite simply, it's me and it wants me. That's it. The work we engage in to uncover our shadows is part of the "doing" – "the work" – we must face. At the same time, total acceptance of our shadows is the "being" we must embrace. My friends, it is by accepting all parts of ourselves that we transform our shadows. *Acceptance is what enables us to transmute the darkness into light.*

## ✳ Reflection Exercise: Hello, Shadow

What is one of your shadows? If you are unsure, think of someone who really annoys you and what the exact quality is that you dislike. For example, maybe you despise "angry" people. Chances are, then, that anger is a quality within yourself that you disown. So you could take a moment to write your thoughts about your relationship with anger.

Keep in mind that not all shadows are "negative" qualities. Some might be positive. For example, maybe you dislike people who are wealthy or successful. If that is the case, take a moment to consider your beliefs around money, success, and power. Notice how you may deny these things for yourself, based on your belief of being worthy. The point is that often what we don't like in another is an aspect of ourselves that we are disowning – or desiring but won't allow ourselves to embrace. Later in the book I will share more about why this is so. For now, simply jot down what comes to mind.

_____

_____

_____

_____

_____

_____

_____

_____

_____

_____

_____

_____

# Transforming Darkness into Light

### Fear and Acceptance

Without acceptance, change isn't possible. Acceptance is what transmutes the darkness into light. When I accepted my shame around the belief that I needed to drink to be able to let go, relax, be myself, and enjoy, I was able to begin the work of shedding that old belief. Yes, a *belief* is what it came down to. This old belief, based entirely in fear, no longer served me. It was a belief I carried with me because I didn't know any other way at the time to deal with the stress of life. Witnessing my father die from what I felt was chronic stress that was not dealt with was enough motivation for me to find another way to peel back the layers of fear and get to the root. That's when I found yoga. Actually, yoga found me!

It is often the case that when the student is ready, the teacher appears. Yoga was, and still is, a profound teacher for me. Yoga gave me the space to get more into my physical body, and it taught me to be gentle with myself as I began to embrace my fear. I learned how to ride the waves of my emotions without getting caught in the drama as often by employing a practice called BRFWA. I learned BRFWA while studying at the Kripalu Center for Yoga and Health, and it is powerful. BRFWA stands for breathe, relax, feel, watch, allow. Here's how it works. As a wave of emotion comes over me, I begin to slow down my *breath*. As my breath slows, my mind and body begin to *relax*. Relaxed, I am able to soften into what I'm *feeling*. While feeling, I am able to *watch* the emotions rather than become them. As I watch, I am able to remain present to *allow* the emotions to flow through me. In this way I am not resisting anything. I am allowing myself the experience of feeling *all* of it fully. By giving the feelings space to flow, they come and go without being all consuming. Over the years, BRFWA has become a powerful and simple awareness practice that quickly brings me back to being present, enabling me to gain perspective and choose wisely.

As I deepened my yoga and meditation practice, I felt I was getting closer to the root of this fear-based belief around having to drink to experience myself fully. However, my intellectual side wasn't satisfied with the idea that the belief simply had to go. I needed, wanted, and longed to understand *why* there was so much fear in the first place. *Why was I so afraid to be who I am?*

Determined to explore this question as part of my life's work, I decided to pursue my yoga teacher training at Kripalu. I felt I needed to immerse myself in the deep inquiry that Kripalu yoga invites. Thus began another phase of intensely beautiful growth. In the years that followed, as my family and friends will attest, I studied everything yoga! I read books, participated in workshops, and pretty much lived, breathed, and ate yoga. Perhaps the most profound lesson from all of this study, if there was one, was that I still had more deep diving to do around the "f" word, *fear*. Among other things, my yoga practice taught me to be compassionate with myself in the unfolding. It wasn't until a few years after I became a yoga teacher that the root of my fear revealed itself. I understand now that yoga was preparing me to receive the information by giving me the necessary tools to handle it. Allow me to explain.

My dedication to yoga drew me to Costa Rica for a yoga retreat. During the retreat I also wanted to experience some pampering! While looking at the brochure, hoping to find a massage, what I found instead would change my life dramatically, yet again. There it was, before my eyes: a shamanic energy healing session. As I read the description, I knew this was "it." This was the doorway I had been searching for. At that point, I had never heard of shamanism. However, I was becoming more curious about the "energy" body and felt energy healing was the next phase of growth for me. For those unfamiliar with shamanic energy healing, here is a brief description from my own website, www. thrivingyouthrivinglife.com, of what a session may entail:

"Shamanic energy sessions are powerful for assisting clients with *big life changes* such as *job transition, marriage & divorce, finding love, death & grief, finding & manifesting one's passion and life calling, developing spiritually, improving health.* A variety of ancient methods are used such as: *Extractions* to release karmic / habitual patterns & energy blocks;

# Reclaiming Joy

*Shamanic Journeying* to meet an ally / gain wisdom from the unseen world; *Soul Retrieval* to restore wholeness and balance to the spirit; *Death Rites* to reset the body."

The shamanic session I had was powerful, and clearly I had much to "release." The practitioner performed the Death Rites on me. She explained that it's not what typically happens in the first session but she felt I was grounded enough to receive. Boy, did I receive! I don't recall much detail about our session; I just knew it was a total reset for my energetic body and the most profound experience I'd had to date. After the session I felt the sheer bliss that, I learned, results from so many years, even lifetimes, of deep release. Then my intellectual brain kicked in and wanted to research shamanism to understand what the heck had happened. This time, instead of giving in to the "doing," I made a different choice. I chose to honor "being" in the bliss of the unknown. I held off doing research until I was back home in New York.

Needless to say, I returned to New York, did my research, and promptly enrolled in a shamanic energy training program. Not only did I feel that shamanic energy healing was the missing piece in my professional practice working with clients, I knew it was what would help me get to the root of my fear once and for all, as well.

As my studies of shamanism deepened, I fell more in love with it. Shamanism is considered to be one of the *most ancient forms of healing* practiced by humans worldwide. Historically, shamanic healing was used by indigenous people from all parts of the world. It made so much sense to me. As I embraced the wisdom of shamanism, I realized that when greeted with a clear intention and motivation for shift, shamanism is a powerful approach to self-discovery that facilitates deep transformation and healing. Right up my alley!

Like I had with yoga, I fully immersed myself in being a student of shamanism. I asked my brain to take a chill pill and practiced "beginner's mind." I let go of what I thought I knew and *allowed* myself to participate in and experience energy clearing rituals, fire ceremonies, and practices of shamanic journeying. I listened intently to the stories of healing and transformation told to me by the shamans. I did what they said. A year later, I had an experience that revealed the root of my fear. There is no question that the shamanic rituals, similar to the practice of yoga, prepared me to receive information I needed to finally let go of my fear in order to fully be myself.

This is what happened. It was a few days after my thirty-ninth birthday, and I was sitting to meditate. At the time, I was feeling tired, frustrated, and sad. I was "beating myself up" and being judgmental. It seemed like I was doing all the right things –meditation, yoga, writing, shamanic healing, working with mentors, etc. – but I still felt unable to fully be myself. Then it happened: I had a spontaneous past-life regression.

In his book *Many Lives, Many Masters* Dr. Brian Weiss shares how he discovered past-life regression to help clients heal current fears and phobias by using hypnosis to take them back to past lives where those things had begun. The reasoning is that by connecting current fears to past lives, often the fear disappears and deep healing occurs. When I had my past-life regression experience, I hadn't yet read that book. I was aware of this concept yet didn't give it much consideration in terms of my own life.

Here are the details of my spontaneous past-life regression: As I mentioned, I was preparing to meditate. I usually meditate with the stones I use for my shamanic healing sessions. For some reason, on this day I was drawn to a stone that my dear friend Rich had brought back from Peru and given me for my birthday a few days earlier. As I meditated, I started tapping my sixth chakra, or third eye, with my finger. The sixth chakra is located between our eyebrows and connects us to our intuition, higher self, and wisdom. I decided to place the stone there. As soon as I did, I had the past-life regression.

The past-life regression happened in a span of about twenty seconds. I saw myself as an infant in a past lifetime in a community where I was regarded as special, a child of light. In the first scene I saw myself as an infant in the arms of one of my parents (which parent exactly wasn't clear). There were no cars at this time, so we were on horseback, when someone came by on another horse and kidnapped me. Flash forward to the next scene, and I was older, a teenager, and was being returned to my parents. Instead of being happy to see me, and welcoming me home, my parents *rejected* me. They didn't want me back because of my specialness. The attention I drew from the community was too much for them to handle.

Then the regression was over. When I came back into my meditation, I heard a voice say to me, "Stephanie, even if you are rejected by everyone, including your parents, I will not ever reject you. Be who you are." I asked myself, whose voice is this? My higher self? God? Both? Yes and yes. I began to sob.

In this twenty-second experience, I got to the long-awaited root of my fear. I realized that up until this past life regression experience, I was still afraid of completely being myself. Based on my experience in a past life, which was buried in my subconscious, there was a *negative consequence for being me*. The original consequence was being rejected by my parents, the very same people who were supposed to love and protect me. It was terrifying! As an adult in this lifetime, I realized that I had been carrying that old fear. Up until the past-life regression, it was a blind spot. Now revealed, it became clear to me that I was afraid that if I stepped fully into my power as a divine feminine creative force and claimed my light, I would be *rejected*. That realization was incredibly freeing and empowering.

The experience of that past-life regression gave me the necessary wisdom, confidence, and, ultimately, healing I needed to fully shed my fear about being who I am. The fatigue, frustration, and sadness I felt that day when I first sat down to meditate transmuted into a deep sense of peace, gratitude, and love. I realized how much of my precious energy I had been giving away to fear over the years. Over the next several months I brought this wisdom into my daily meditation practice by repeating the statement I had heard: "Stephanie, even if you are rejected by everyone, including your parents, I will not ever reject you. Be who you are." I did this until I believed it and started being who I was without the fear of rejection. Was it easy? At first, no way. Discomfort became a very familiar feeling. I stayed with the discomfort, though, practicing BRFWA often, because I knew there was no alternative. I was done with hiding behind fear. I wanted to be me!

Looking back, I see that in order to fully let go of my fear I had to make sense of it on an intellectual level and also release it at the energetic level. It wasn't enough to have one or the other. I needed *both*. This is why I am so passionate about yoga and shamanic energy healing as powerful tools for healing. Together they provide awareness to satisfy the mind and body and rituals to clear the energy.

During this process another powerful piece of wisdom was revealed to me – that each and every one of us is love and light. Love and light are at the core of our being. *What does this mean?* It means that we are *not* actually transforming the darkness into light, per se. *What we are really transforming is our perspective, and therefore our thoughts, about darkness itself and who we are.*

At our core we are light, not dark. While we may have shadow aspects of ourselves that we consider to be dark, this is *not* who we are. As we stay committed to reclaiming joy, and as we live as joy by allowing ourselves to be who we really are, we realize the light is always there. The light patiently waits for us to stop, look, and listen – to stop driving and start thriving. The light is what pulls us forward. The light is what illuminates the dark. And, yes, we do need both. We would not "know" one without the other. My friends, it is in the space of *acceptance* where we transform our perspective and therefore our thoughts of darkness into light.

## ❉ Reflection Exercise: Love and Light

Think of someone – alive or deceased – who represents love and light to you. List a few of their qualities. Of those, which ones do you already see in yourself?

Which ones do you want to cultivate?

_____

_____

_____

_____

_____

_____

_____

## Lessons of Light

### Meaning, Forgiveness, Healing, Empowerment

As we begin to practice acceptance (yes, it's an on-going practice, not something that will ever be perfect) it's necessary to find *meaning* in what we have experienced. Why? We will face moments when we want to give up. This is normal. When we find meaning, it helps to keep us motivated, so we stay open to learning and growing. Finding meaning also gives us hope. Hope is important, because it renews our faith in the human spirit long enough to give us an opportunity to rise again. Upon rising we begin to learn about the power of forgiveness on the path to reclaiming joy.

As we practice reclaiming joy, the importance of *forgiveness is revealed*. The truth is, without the ability to forgive, it is hard to fully accept. If we don't fully accept, we will find ourselves back in the same place we were trying to move forward from. Like meaning, forgiveness gives us the opportunity to *honor and integrate* all we have experienced so we stay committed to the path. Forgiveness helps ease the pain we experience when bad things happen. What I find so humbling about learning to forgive is that *often the first person we have to forgive is ourselves*. Why? Read on.

As I've shared previously, while doing my shadow work on why I was using alcohol to relax, a lot of shame came up for me. I felt ashamed that

I had to use something to have a good time. This brought up feelings of weakness and helplessness. In my daily life, weak and helpless were not the images I wanted to portray, at all. I'd been determined not ever to be "helpless." Since my childhood, I had prided myself on being the strong, smart, reliable person whom people looked to for advice. Because of that, people naturally came to expect that I would *always* be that way. What a responsibility! This coupled with the fear of letting go of that facade, which was also my identity, was terrifying. As I worked through the truth of where I was (using alcohol to relax) and began to accept it, I realized I had to forgive myself in order to fully integrate the experience and move forward.

Forgiveness became a portal that allowed me to really see with authenticity who I was *being* and *why*. As I forgave myself, the shame began to soften. In the softening, my compassion toward myself began to grow. Have you ever noticed that compassion is like a muscle? The more we work it, the stronger it gets. As our compassion grows, we can see ourselves with greater love and acceptance. When we see ourselves through the eyes of love, instead of the lens of shame and judgment, it is much easier, and far more enjoyable, to learn and grow.

In my case, what I learned while doing shadow work was that the shame around feeling weak and helpless served me well for some time by helping me to discover my gifts. Feeling shame and weak motivated me to focus my energy on being "better". In essence I channeled my energy to cultivate my strength, discipline and independence, the gifts, which ultimately led to my success, and more gifts. In the process, yes, I was successful on the outside. I learned valuable skills that still serve me well to this day. However, I also learned that working from shame wasn't sustainable or joyful. Working from a place of "not being enough" meant endless doing, doing, and more doing. It was exhausting. My shame, once met with acceptance, love, compassion, and forgiveness, taught me that all of my doing wasn't supporting my being.

When I realized the disconnect between wanting to be joy and acting in a way that did not support joy, I was able to make sense of *why* I was doing what I was doing and honor that. I shifted from being in shame and judgment to being grateful for the lessons and humbled for my hard work. My perspective shifted from seeing myself as dark to seeing myself as full of light. It was a touch of grace to experience this shift in perspective. I felt immense compassion for myself for all the times I beat myself up with judgment, negative self-talk, and endless doing. I was also able to honor the places I had been and integrate the experiences I'd had. I saw that there was meaning in *all* of it. Nothing was wasted, not even the suffering. From this place of forgiveness I was able to learn the hard lessons and recommit to my personal growth.

As you see, forgiveness is powerful. It sets the ball in motion. Without the ability to forgive myself for where I was and where I had been, I would not have had the necessary ingredients of compassion, love, wisdom, energy, desire, and confidence to get where my spirit longed to go and be who I wanted to be, which was joy. Once the ball was in motion, I was able to stand back and witness my life to determine what was important to my well-being. It was at this point that I began to focus again on the four foundations of well-being that I shared in chapter 1: health, relationship, career, and life purpose.

Today I am still strong, independent, and successful. I love being in action in the world. But there are differences. For example, when I feel helpless, instead of making it shameful, I ask for help. When I feel needy, I do something to nurture myself or reach out to a loved one. When I feel like I am not having success with something, I give it space. Instead of beating myself up, I ask if I am on the right track. If the answer is yes, I ask for and get the support I need.

Looking back, a large part of my growth has come from being able to admit that I *need support* in my life. Perhaps some of you relate to this and are nodding in agreement. Excellent! Whether the support comes from a mentor or coach or from a loved one, the ability to admit that you need help and then ask for it is powerful. I no longer see asking for help as a sign of weakness. In fact, I see asking for help as a sign of wisdom and strength.

Today there is also a difference in *why* I do what I do. In the past, my actions were often motivated by feelings of shame, lack, helplessness, and not being enough. The intentions behind my actions were to do more in order to be better and therefore feel better. My focus was on *doing* to get specific results. Today, my actions are motivated by joy. My focus is on *being* joy. I am still in action and doing. But the intentions behind my actions are to bring more joy – health, happiness, peace, love, and connection – into the world. As a result, I experience life with more ease, gratitude, and grace. I am living as joy.

Are you starting to see the power of forgiveness on the path to reclaiming joy? Forgiveness opens the door to deep healing and transformation. It enables us to grow as we learn about ourselves and accept who we are. Over time, as we stay open and recommit to the path, we begin to gain self-mastery. We learn from our mistakes and change our behavior. We *consciously choose* how we want to experience the world. Do we want to feel love or hate? We begin to understand how we are *being*, which starts on the inside and is reflected in how we *experience* our world on the outside. In this way, as life rolls on, and challenges arise, we decide how we will ride our journey. As we do, it becomes quite apparent that the war we have been waging all along is a war within ourselves.

The realization that the war is within was another game-changing moment in my life. It helped me understand the power of our mind to create madness and therefore unnecessary suffering. It became clear that without gaining mastery of our mind, we will endure much unnecessary suffering and the war within will never stop! We will continue driving hard and miss our chance to thrive. My desire was and is to live a meaningful, worthwhile, and fulfilling life. This desire coupled with my devotion to being a teacher and student of yoga led me to read books on the topic. One of my favorites, The Bhagavad Gita, particularly the translation by Eknath Easwaran, talks about the power of meditation to help us cultivate a mind that is like a steady flame. When meditation is mastered, we don't suffer the afflictions of a wavering, restless, monkey mind. We are no longer swept back and forth by the pain and pleasure of life. Instead, we are steady, rooted, and grounded in ourselves. We are present for our life, and we are able to experience fulfillment.

When we arrive at this steady place, even for a short time, we can look at all of our experiences as teachings. We become compassionate witnesses to our own life. In doing that, we hold the more difficult and painful experiences (and ourselves) in reverence rather than shame. We become less affected by the push-pull, light-dark, right-wrong, good-bad – the aversion-attraction dance, as I sometimes call it. We simply *notice*. In this way, we begin to understand that *nothing is wasted*. Any suffering we have endured is all nectar for our growth – a reminder that freedom, like joy, is a state of being. It's pretty incredible, really. Consider it. As we embrace the practice of looking at all our *experiences as teachers*, our experiences no longer have to bind us. We are free to choose how we "hold" them in our awareness. If we choose to be free, we learn to see our experiences as happening *for* us instead of *to* us. We move from a place of being disempowered (victim) to being empowered. I don't know about you, but when I feel empowered, I feel free. I am not bound by anything (fear!) or anyone (those who represent fear). I am myself. I am unstoppable, expansive, and my heart is open to receive. Like joy, freedom is a choice. What will you choose?

As we choose freedom, we also choose the path of *empowerment*. And as we choose empowerment, we continue strengthening our compassion muscle. Think about it. If we are judging and engaging in negative self-talk, both disempowering behaviors, how can we be free? On the other hand, when we choose to be compassionate toward ourselves, we witness instead of judge. We engage in positive self-talk. We end up feeling empowered. This doesn't happen without compassion. As self-compassion grows, we are better able to extend compassion to *others*. In doing that, we prepare ourselves for the process of *extending forgiveness to those who have hurt us*. My friends, this is where ever more joy and freedom await.

As I shared in chapter 1, relationships are foundational to well-being on the path to reclaiming joy. When we go through life unable to forgive others for the pain they have "caused" us, we live with that pain in some way by holding on to it. Deep down inside of us, until we fully release the pain, by way of forgiveness, it keeps us bound, the opposite of free.

Perhaps our painful experiences have caused us not to trust people, life itself, or even ourselves. We live in fear. Fear contracts us. To keep ourselves "safe," we close our hearts, thinking that is the solution. In the short term, perhaps that is what we need to do. In the long run, however, it doesn't serve us. When we live in fear mode, with a closed heart, it is hard to be who we are, which is love and light. Living in fear keeps us disempowered, bound, and we aren't free. We live behind the walls we've constructed. Remember those? The walls keep out connection, intimacy, joy. To reclaim joy is to choose freedom. *In choosing freedom, we are invited to forgive those who have caused us the most pain.*

Some of you might be having a strong reaction to these words right now, especially those who have experienced abuse, violence, or trauma of any kind. It may seem impossible to imagine having compassion, let alone extending forgiveness, to someone who has hurt or violated you. Be aware of your body in this moment. If you need to pause, honor yourself and come back to this part when you are ready. What I will share is an invitation for you to consider a perspective I gained a few years back on the ability to extend compassion and forgiveness to those who have hurt others.

On the same yoga retreat where I discovered shamanism, I had the privilege of attending a discussion on compassion hosted by Joan Halifax, an American Zen Buddhist teacher. She was talking about her work with prisoners on death row. As she was sharing, I remember feeling awestruck by her ability to be so compassionate and forgiving to people who had committed such atrocious acts. My heart wanted to close in anger many times, yet I chose to stay open. I was there for a reason and knew if I got into anger mode, I wouldn't receive the lesson. Eventually, someone was brave enough to ask, "How do you do it?" Her answer forever changed my perspective on the power of compassion and forgiveness. She said, "Anger and violence are a form of helplessness. Those hardest to love need love the most."

There it was! That word *helplessness* again – one of my shadows. Immediately, my heart melted in compassion for those she served on death row. Her wisdom challenged me and ultimately allowed me to see that I am really not so different from "them." How so? I chose to turn my helplessness into violence against *myself* by hard driving, judging, and doing the "not enough" dance that resulted in excessive drinking, eating, working, etc. They chose to turn their helplessness into violence against *others*. Some of you may be saying there is no comparison. Perhaps not. Yet we all know people who violently abuse their bodies in ways that cause them to die or come pretty close. My point is, it is so easy to judge others.

When we practice BRFWA, stand back, and see what is beneath the surface, it becomes startlingly clear that we are the *same* at our core. We are all love and light, remember? How we act out when we forget this is what makes us "look" different to others. Listening to Joan Halifax was a most humbling experience that opened my eyes to the power and necessity of compassion and forgiveness on the path to reclaiming joy. *As we embark on the path to reclaiming joy, we embark on the journey of healing.*

Part of healing is the ability to have compassion and forgive while looking at *all experiences* as our teachers. As we do this, we begin to understand the role other people (and their stories), no matter how painful, play in our journey. Their story is our story. Their lessons are our lessons. All experience paves the way for our learning and, in turn, our healing, if we choose to see it as such. In her book *Aphrodite's Daughters*, author Jalaja Bonheim says, "The unspeakable cruelty of life cannot be rationalized. Abuse remains abuse, torture remains torture, and suffering remains suffering. Yet the descent, if approached as a call to a healing journey, can lead to a place where, without denying the darkness, we nonetheless praise the goodness of life." The universe wants *all* of us to heal, not just some of us. We will continue to find ourselves in similar situations until we learn the lesson. We know we have learned when we *choose differently* and therefore find ourselves in a different situation.

My friends, the invitation to extend compassion and forgiveness beyond ourselves is so that we may heal. *When we heal, we are free to be who we are.* When we heal, we reclaim joy. Perhaps most profound as it relates to this being human is that when we heal, we give someone else the opportunity to heal, as well. We give someone else the freedom to be who THEY are. We invite them to walk with us on the path to reclaim joy. Imagine a world with all of us being joy. Now, that is something to get excited about!

### ✳ Reflection Exercise: Forgiveness Letter

Create a nourishing atmosphere for yourself. Light a candle, put on some music, shut off all high-tech devices. Write a brief letter to someone in your life whom you want to forgive. Remember that this person may be you. After you write the letter, burn it. The element of fire transmutes the energy. To prepare, take a moment to write your thoughts here about who and what needs forgiveness.

_____

_____

_____

_____

_____

_____

_____

## Chapter Summary and Reflection

In this chapter I spoke about what gets in the way of us experiencing joy and how we can empower ourselves by looking at our experiences as teachers. Specifically, I shared the value of shadow work and how it is an ongoing and powerful practice on the path to reclaiming joy. I discussed how fear often keeps us stuck and explained the role acceptance plays in allowing us to move forward in pursuing the life we desire. Finally, I spoke of the importance of forgiveness and how it is often ourselves we need to forgive first. Ultimately, as we dive deep into ourselves and practice acceptance and forgiveness, we empower ourselves to reclaim joy.

At the start of this chapter I invited you to have faith. When we begin to face the darker aspects of ourselves, which we considered in this chapter, it often brings up many emotions. Without judgment, simply notice how you are feeling with this material. Exhale. Practice being a witness. Practice being compassion. As I mentioned previously, on the road to reclaiming joy, at times it may feel anything but joyful. Yet, if you recall, joy is a state of being, right? That means we are still joy even when we experience fear or anger or sadness. My wish for you at this point is to learn the value of forgiveness and healing and the freedom it creates for you to be yourself. By fully embracing this freedom, you are invited to reclaim your power in support of your journey to reclaim joy – your journey to be YOU.

*"The Voice-induced decisions – those made from shame and force, guilt or deprivation, cannot be trusted. They do not last because they are based on fear of consequences instead of longing for truth. Instead, ask yourself what you love. Without fear of consequences, without force or shame or guilt. What motivates you to be kind, to take care of your body, your spirit, others, the earth? Trust the longing, trust the love that can be translated into action without the threat of punishment. Trust that you will not destroy what matters most. Give yourself that much."*

—*Geneen Roth*, Women, Food, and God

## CHAPTER THREE

# Following Your Joy

*"Comparison is the thief of joy."*
—Eleanor Roosevelt

# Reclaiming Joy

Well done. You have gotten so far already! I trust you have read the previous chapters and perhaps even completed some or all of the exercises. Bravo. Give yourself two gold stars. If you haven't, pause and consider why not? Maybe this chapter will give you the nectar needed to return to the previous chapters and exercises. Rest assured, whatever you do, it's perfect. You are here now, reading this, and that is a big step!

In the previous two chapters the focus has been on raising awareness about what it means to reclaim joy. In chapter 1 we defined joy, discussed the four foundations for joy (health, relationship, career, life purpose) and posed the question, Is joy a choice?

In chapter 2, we dove deep and looked at what gets in the way of reclaiming joy. We explored our shadows and looked at how we transmute darkness into light by shifting our perspective and therefore our thoughts. We examined the power of acceptance and forgiveness as they relate to growth, healing, and, ultimately, our collective empowerment.

By now my hope is that you are building your foundation of awareness for what reclaiming joy looks like in your *unique* life. This foundation will support you in moving on to the next phase, which is taking inspired action and following your joy.

Take a moment to pause. Inhale deeply. Exhale deeply. Do that again. One more time. Now acknowledge yourself for *showing up*. Didn't that feel good? As our journey together continues, in this chapter I will outline what is required for you to be successful in following your joy. By the end of this chapter my intention is for you to be aware of the magical dance between *what you are doing* and *how you are being* in your practice of reclaiming joy. By which I mean, are your thoughts, words, and actions aligned?

## Grounding

### Relaxed Mind, Balanced Emotions

Would you agree that if you are traveling to a new place having a GPS or map of *how* to get there would be helpful? For most of us the answer is yes, especially if getting there is important. If we really want something, we want the most efficient, direct route to get it. This doesn't mean we stay on course the entire way. It simply means we have put *thought* into where we want to go and the *possible* ways to get there. We are aware. With awareness we are able to make *conscious* choices. So if we decide to go off course, or something causes us to go off course, we have the ability to stay present and pay attention. The same principle applies to reclaiming joy. If you really want to live as joy, whatever that means for unique you, a map of possible ways to arrive at that state of being will help support your journey.

Take a moment to notice your reaction to the preceding paragraph. Does the idea of mapping out your journey make you feel excited and expansive? Nervous and contracted? Simply watch without judgment. I bring this up to illustrate a point. In my experience, success in life requires enlisting our mind to work in concert with our emotions. For a very long time, I was *totally resistant* to having any sort of map or plan. I lived in the space of emotion, and while I had thoughts of using a map, I felt all would "work out" if I simply set the intention. Guess what? That method didn't work out so well!

After admitting I was not where I wanted to be, my shadow and shamanic work revealed doubt and fear were at the root of the resistance. I was resistant to do the work of mapping, which I now call visualization. I will discuss visualization in more detail later. What I want to share now is that I was living so much in my emotional body, I was terrified to put my dreams of the life I imagined out there. As is usually the case, fear put doubt in my mind. I simply didn't think the life I imagined for myself was *possible*.

Think about it. *It takes courage to create a really big map that includes really big dreams.* When we do, we are also subconsciously committing ourselves to stand in our power and shine our light. For many of us, myself included, this brings up all things related to fear, as I shared in the last chapter. As we have learned, the only way to live the life of our dreams is by working through any resistance. Remember that resistance is the universe at work, conspiring on our behalf, encouraging us to shine. Perhaps Marianne Williamson says it best in her book A Return to Love: Reflections on the Principles of "A Course in Miracles":

*"Our deepest fear is not that we are inadequate. Our deepest fear is that we are powerful beyond measure. It is our light, not our darkness that most frightens us. We ask ourselves, Who am I to be brilliant, gorgeous, talented, fabulous? Actually, who are you not to be? You are a child of God. Your playing small does not serve the world. There is nothing enlightened about shrinking so that other people won't feel insecure around you. We are all meant to shine, as children do. We were born to make manifest the glory of God that is within us. It's not just in some of us; it's in everyone. And as we let our own light shine, we unconsciously give other people permission to do the same. As we are liberated from our own fear, our presence automatically liberates others."*

Take a moment to notice how you are *feeling* after reading that quote. If you are like me, maybe you are joyfully shouting, YES!! It makes sense, doesn't it? Who are we *not* to live the life of our dreams? Why else are we here? What I find particularly heartwarming in reading that quote is that living *our* dreams is not an either-or proposition. When I live the life of my dreams, I don't take away that possibility from someone else. You *and* I live our dreams, not you *or* I. Magnificent, really. The "or" comes into play only when we are living from the "not enough" mentality, which I was doing. When we shift our perspective, and begin to live from the wealth mentality, we see that there is *more than enough* for all of us to live our dreams. This taught me the power of connecting and aligning what I envisioned for my life to my emotional body. It got me interested in learning how to live from *balanced* emotion, rather than only emotion. That helped me begin to make changes in my life to support reclaiming joy. Let me explain how it works.

In my quest to cultivate *emotional balance* and therefore make changes, I turned to the book *Switch: How to Change Things When Change Is Hard* by Chip and Dan Heath. The book uses the analogy of the roles of an elephant and rider to illustrate making deep and lasting change. The elephant represents emotion, or how we are being. The rider represents the mind, or what we are doing. In life, we need both emotion and the mind. We need emotion to "buy into" a vision; we need the mind to execute that vision. *However, in any given moment, the elephant (emotion) can crush the rider (mind).* In my own life, I have seen how overwhelming, unregulated emotion will quickly derail me from my vision, shutting me down completely. Emotion is sometimes simply too powerful for the mind to overcome. With this understanding and my ability to stay aware, present, and compassionate, I have learned how to balance my emotional state in order to stay true to myself on the path to reclaiming joy.

How do we balance our emotional state? The first step is to practice awareness and acceptance. Sound familiar? Before we balance anything, we have to authentically recognize and *accept* our current emotional state or mood. Remember that what we resist will persist. Once we choose to acknowledge and accept where we find ourselves, then we move forward to step two.

In step two we regulate our emotions. For me, the easiest and quickest way to regulate how I am "being" in the moment is by taking a *movement or meditation break.* Typically, when my emotions are out of balance, I feel energy surging through my body, and it needs to be released with movement. (I have to move my body moderately to vigorously five days a week anyway to feel balanced overall.) When I need to take a quick movement break in the midst of my day, I practice a few minutes of intense yoga breathing with postures or go for a power walk outdoors. If my mind is scattered and that's affecting my emotions, I opt for meditation and breath work, instead. One of my favorite breathing techniques called Nadi Shodhana (Alternate Nostril Breathing) works well for this. I'll share how to practice that at the end of this section.

Whether I choose movement or meditation, what results is a shift in energy from being stuck to feeling free. As the energy shifts, emotions come back into balance, and the mind is restored to a state of peace.

# Reclaiming Joy

From that place of *balanced emotion* and *relaxed mind* we are able to return to the place of *possibility* and set in motion what we envision. The next section will address the next set of ingredients required to be successful in following our joy – visualization and action.

## ❈ Breathing Exercise: Nadi Shodhana Pranayama

Practice Nadi Shodhana pranayama (alternate nostril breathing; *nadi* = subtle energy channel; *shodhan* = cleaning, purification; *pranayama* = breathing technique) to calm the body and mind and balance the emotions.

**Here's how:** Sitting comfortably with a straight spine, relaxed shoulders, and a softened face, rest your left hand, palm up, on your left knee. Raise your right hand and bring your ring finger and thumb to rest on your left and right nostrils, respectively. Press your thumb down to close the right nostril and breathe in slowly through the left nostril. Press your ring finger down on your left nostril, lift your thumb and breathe out slowly through the right. Now breathe in slowly through the right nostril, switch fingers, and breathe out through the left. Repeat this cycle of alternate nostril breathing for ten cycles, or longer as desired. Keep your eyes closed and breathe slowly and easily throughout.

You can use this technique before bed to help you sleep, throughout the day to keep you grounded, even during a bathroom break if you're overwhelmed at work! Because this technique is so effective at clearing out blocked energy channels in the body, it's also a great way to prepare your mind and body for your meditation practice. After you try this exercise, write down what your experience was like here. What did you notice? How do you feel?

_____

_____

_____

_____

_____

_____

# Getting There

### Visualization, Action

Enlisting our relaxed mental body to work with our balanced emotional body is part of the process of reclaiming joy that supports us in taking action toward what we want to manifest. In my experience both with myself and in working with clients, there is a tendency at times to get *so overwhelmed* with the idea of "starting" something that we end up doing *nothing*. We get so paralyzed about taking the perfect or right action in pursuit of our dreams that we take no action at all. Do you relate? Why does this happen?

For most of us it comes down to fear. When we dream and then begin to think about our dreams, we innocently believe we must have it all figured out in terms of "how." This frightens us. In addition, many of us are impatient, to boot. We have an expectation that as soon as we decide to make changes, the results ought to hurry up and arrive! When they don't come as fast as we want, we begin thinking, "I don't have what it takes to make this happen" or "It's not meant to be." When doubt creeps in, we lose precious energy and motivation. The doubt takes us out of action. This cycle of fear, doubt, and inaction prevents us from making changes and living the life of our dreams. Thankfully, there is a solution. *As quickly as doubt takes us out of action, action takes us out of doubt.* My friends, *we must learn to doubt the doubt so we stay in action!* Let's face it, doubt also makes our journey far less joyful, and we are here to be joy, yes?

If I were a betting woman, I'd bet you are now wondering, "How do we doubt the doubt so that we stay in action?" So happy you asked! The answer is giving yourself permission to use your imagination, also known as the practice of visualization. Truth be told, I didn't understand the power of visualization until fairly recently. In the past, perhaps like some of you, I had done my share of vision boards. I cut out pictures of words and images that appealed to me and pasted them on a board. I hung the boards somewhere visible, lit a candle, and set an intention for things to "happen." I *waited* for my life to shift. Guess what? Not much happened. It wasn't until I began deepening my shamanic practices and then found Mike Dooley's DVD *Thoughts Become Things* that I began to understand the *power of visualization* when done properly. In his DVD, Dooley gives easy-to-use visualization guidelines that work. He explains the synergistic effect of combining visualization with taking action in order to manifest our dreams. He also shares how our thoughts and words create our reality and emphasizes how to use and not use them.

What is it about visualization that is so powerful? In my experience, visualization teaches us how to strengthen our five senses and expand our imagination to receive wisdom. Visualization is a practice that invites us to *go beyond* our limited mind. In doing that, we move from living in "probability" (doubt lives there) to living in "possibility" (where we are unstoppable). When living in possibility, we do things we might not otherwise, even if – especially if – those things don't make *sense*.

On the shamanic path, staying opening to possibility is part of the ongoing practice. The more in tune I am with what I am hearing, seeing, tasting, smelling, and feeling, the more wisdom I receive about what actions to take. What is revealed to me in the form of words, images, and sounds is often beyond what my mind alone is capable of grasping. Meaning, no thinking would lead me to what I was being shown, because what I was being shown wasn't "logical" at the moment.

I suspect some of you already know what I'm talking about, yes? Perhaps you look back at an aspect of your life that you've been able to manifest in a BIG way and realize all the people, places, and situations that *aligned* to get you there. At the time, perhaps the actions you took didn't seem perfect or right. Yet something beyond your mind inspired you to take those actions. As you did, a window or door opened, or a path was revealed, and you were successful. Miraculous, yes! *When we let go of doubt and connect to divine intelligence that exists beyond our limited mind, we open ourselves up to infinite possibilities.* At the same time, with the universe conspiring on our behalf, we will be "rewarded" for our actions.

Do you see what I'm saying? In order to get what we want, we must stay in action. In order to stay in action, we must practice doubting our doubt by using visualization. When we practice visualization "properly," we have to "lose our mind" and connect to our senses. The reality is, our mind is what limits us by instilling doubt and worrying about "how" something will happen. As we practice visualization, we must let go of "how" in order to go beyond our mind. When we do, we are able to imagine what is possible, which enables us to connect to the *energy* of our imagination. The energy of our imagination is powerful – it *inspires* us to act! The energy of doubt shuts us down. Still doubtful? Let's look at an example of how attaching to "how" limits us.

Imagine one of your dreams is to create a lifestyle in which you work for yourself from home generating a significant income. Presently, you are working for someone else. One day you find yourself feeling very relaxed, and you decide to practice visualization. As you let yourself go, your mind relaxes and your imagination begins to run wild with possibilities. You see your house and you working in it generating a significant income. You connect to your senses and feel excited – lit up! The possibility ignites you from the inside out. You feel the energy of action in your belly. You continue this journey for a few minutes, and then suddenly that voice in your head starts saying, "You are crazy! Not going to happen. How is that even possible? You live paycheck to paycheck! You don't have the money to start a business. Besides, you never ran your own business and you don't have the skills." And so on. Frustrated, you agree with your mind and stop imagining. You believe what your mind is telling you and buy into its limited nature. You shut down. You feel lousy. The energy of action in your belly turns to tension, and you feel afraid. You are no longer inspired to take action.

This example illustrates how quickly doubt will take us out of action. In order to practice visualization effectively it's important to understand two things. First, as you are visualizing, you must be willing to release the "how." Second, as you visualize, you must connect emotionally.

# Reclaiming Joy

As you saw in the example above, when we release the "how," our imagination is free to run wild with possibility. We are unstoppable, and we stay in the flow! As we experience the *energy* of possibility by releasing how, we then connect emotionally by using all of our senses. As we tap into the energy of possibility, we will feel motivated to take action in the direction of our dreams. Our emotions are powerful, remember? The elephant (emotions) and rider (mind) example I shared earlier illustrates that when we connect to the emotion of possibility, we energize ourselves to take action. Remember that the ingredients for success are *visualization plus action*.

Here's an example of *effective* visualization I used to help me to write and publish this, my first book, in less than eight months. I promise you, my mind did not think it was possible at all. In my *daily* visualization practice I gave myself the freedom to imagine endless possibility. I didn't worry about how, and I connected emotionally to what I visualized. I practiced seeing myself in action *after* the book was published. I visualized myself on stage discussing my book with people excited to read it. I felt the warmth of the spotlight on my face. I saw the faces of people in the audience. I heard their clapping and their voices saying thank you. I smelled the pages of the book and saw the front cover on a billboard. I saw myself being interviewed by Oprah and doing Ted Talks – being received with a standing ovation. I heard people inviting me to lead a retreat based on this book in a warm climate in the middle of New York winter. Talk about lit up—I would be buzzing.

In the process of these visualizations I connected to what it *felt* like, as if all of it was *already* happening. Again, I didn't worry about how. How did it make me feel? Amazed, humbled, energized, and inspired! My visualization experiences added fuel to my energetic fire, so that I stayed in action and on track with finishing this book by my "aggressive" deadline. It also kept me totally excited, open, and interested in the possibilities of what's to come.

Visualization practices can be used for anything you desire, such as cultivating love relationships. Let's take another example. Imagine you want a love relationship. You have done your inner work and are now ready and available to welcome your life partner, your beloved. Totally exciting. Start by taking these two steps:

First, begin to visualize yourself in that relationship. See yourself doing things you enjoy together. Fully engage your senses and create an emotional connection. Let go of how. How does it make you feel? Are you feeling energized and inspired to act? Great!

Second, decide to take one action in support of your desire. One simple action might be telling your best friend in advance about the person you're inviting into your life and all of the things you will do together. Describe this person and the scene in such detail that you begin to tap into the energy. Another action may be to write a letter to the universe thanking it in advance for sending you this person.

Remember the key to success is *not getting caught up* in the notion that there is some *perfect or right action* that will take you from where you are presently to where you want to go. That is simply *not* the case. Focus instead on using your visualization practice to allow your imagination to run wild and connect emotionally to what you sense. Doing that will give you the necessary fuel to take *inspired action* while putting you in a position to be moved effortlessly along the path to reclaiming joy via divine intelligence, or the power beyond your mind. Note that I used the term "*inspired* action" this time. I'll explain more about this in the next section. For now keep in mind that the formula for success in manifesting the life you want is visualization plus action.

## ✳ Visualization Exercise: Use Your Imagination

Choose one foundational area of your life that you want to focus on. What is it you desire in this area? Once you set your intention, set a timer for five minutes. Release the how, and let your imagination run wild with possibility. Connect to all of your senses. What do you see, hear, smell, taste? Feel everything, including the energy of possibility. After the five minutes is up, notice how you feel. Take a few minutes to answer the following questions: What did you learn about releasing the how and the power of visualization? What is one action you will take as a result of this experience?

_____

_____

_____

_____

_____

_____

_____

_____

# Inspired Action

### Inner Alignment

By now most of you understand the importance of taking action in support of your vision for reclaiming joy. Maybe you even believe it when I say the action doesn't have to be perfect or right. Getting caught up in worrying whether the action is perfect or right is self-defeating. It drains your energy and will take you *out* of action. Don't get me wrong – I'm not saying that if you want to lose weight to go ahead and keep eating whatever you feel like and expect results. What I am saying is that as you bring your attention to the areas in your life that are calling out to you, you have the opportunity to take actions that bring you closer to living the life you envision. As your attention expands and grows, you will likely be more intentional about your actions. You will begin to notice what actions to take in support of your vision. Action we take from this place of attention and intention I call *inspired action.* In my experience, inspired action, rather than perfect or right action, moves us closer to the life we envision.

Inspired actions are those taken *in support of and aligned with* the vision we have for our life. When our vision is based on *who we are* and *why we are here,* it inspires us to act. Inspired action occurs when what we think, and what we say, is revealed in what we do. Inspired action is fueled by awareness, passion, and integrity, to name a few. When we take inspired action, we are aligned internally. Our thoughts and words are aligned to support our actions, and we feel energized. On the path to reclaiming joy, *being aligned in thought and word to support our actions is essential.* Why do I say this?

As I mentioned in chapter 1, my life purpose fuels my actions and sustains me by giving meaning to my life. When I lose my way, my life purpose helps me return home to myself, back to being joy. In fact, my life purpose *is* the vision I have for my life. I use the words *life purpose* and *vision* interchangeably. Thus, when my vision is clear, my thoughts and words support the inspired actions I take to manifest my life purpose.

Here's an example from my own life. My life purpose is to be a conduit for helping others experience the freedom of being who they are by teaching them to reclaim joy. My *thoughts* support this vision. I *think* about how many people I have already helped reclaim joy. I *think* about fun and inspiring ways to best deliver my message. In addition to my thoughts, my *words* align with this vision. When I *speak*, I talk about how joyful it is to witness clients speaking their voice and setting boundaries in support of being who they are. I *speak* about my desire to share my reclaiming joy mentoring program virtually to reach millions of people worldwide. With my thoughts and words aligned, I am fired up. I feel energized, and I am excited to take inspired actions in support of my vision. It doesn't even feel like work. It feels like joy because I am being me. My doing supports my being and vice versa.

On the other hand, if my thoughts and words are not aligned, and I don't think it's possible for me to be a conduit, yet I tell others that is what I do, it will be impossible to take inspired action for long. Further, when I do act, people will sense something isn't aligned. As a result it will be hard for me to be myself, to be joy, and I certainly won't be acting in service to others. Does this make sense? The key is to check in with our thoughts and words to make sure they align with our vision. Again, it's an awareness practice. When we do this on a regular basis, we free up our energy to take inspired action.

# Reclaiming Joy

As we take inspired action, the people around us *feel* it. You know the type of person I am talking about, right? Some of you are that person already! We all have the ability to do this. When we are aligned and taking inspired action, we become like a magnet and begin to attract what we envision. The universe (yes!) conspires on our behalf to bring to us what we once thought impossible with the utmost ease and grace. The result is that we begin to naturally live in balance or right relationship to ourselves and the world around us.

In the shamanic tradition, the word *Ayni* that describes this state of being. For me, Ayni occurs when our thoughts, words, and actions are aligned. We give and we receive in a balanced manner. Another way I like to think of it is our mind working in concert with our heart to take action in the world. When we live in Ayni, life seems to flow effortlessly. As we affirm the support of the universe, we also raise our energetic vibration or the signal we are sending out. This signal in combination with our aligned thoughts and words provides us the necessary fuel (energy, wisdom, resources) to take inspired action – to follow our joy.

## ✳ Reflection Exercise: Check Your Alignment

Take a few moments to reflect on how or where in your life, in one of your foundational areas (health, relationships, career, life purpose), you are *not* living aligned with thought, word, and action. Meaning, your mind tells you one thing, you say something else, and your action doesn't align with either. For example, perhaps you are ready to let go of a toxic relationship that no longer supports you. Deep down you know the relationship needs to end, and your mind tells you it is toxic. Yet when this person reaches out to you, you continue to say yes when you mean no. You give this person your energy and then you resent it.

Write your answers to the following questions:

What needs to shift or what choices do you need to make for you to create inner alignment? Is there one inspired action you will take to support that shift or those choices?

_____

_____

_____

_____

_____

_____

_____

_____

## Chapter Summary and Reflection

This chapter outlined what is required for you to be successful in following your joy. We discussed the importance of enlisting your mind (rider) and your emotions (elephant) to work together in bringing your vision to reality. We spoke about the power of visualization and developing your senses to help you open more fully to possibility. We shared how staying in action takes you out of doubt and keeps you motivated. Finally, we discussed the power of aligning your thoughts with your words, so that you take *inspired actions*. When all three are aligned – thoughts, words, and actions – you gain the necessary fuel (energy and wisdom) to stay on the path to reclaiming joy.

In the next chapter I will give more specifics about what inspired actions to start taking *now* in order to set yourself up for success. First, pause. Take a deep breath in through your nose. Exhale out of your mouth with a sigh. Know that you already have everything you need within you to be successful.

*"What you do speaks so loudly I can't hear what you say."*

—Anonymous

# Chapter Four
# Living As Joy

*"The journey of a thousand miles begins with the first step."*

—Tao Te Ching

# Reclaiming Joy

In the previous chapter I spoke about what is required to be successful in following our joy – in getting what we want. Let's face it, most of us are impatient, especially when we desire something we feel will bring us "pleasure." With that in mind, this chapter will outline practical ways for you to start living as joy, now. In the pages that follow I will share tips on how to get started, as well as the importance of knowing yourself, and the role of commitment and discipline. I will talk about the meaning of surrender and how to keep the process of reclaiming joy in motion as you continue to grow ever more aware.

By the end of the chapter my intention is for you to gain clarity on what to *do* and to be fiercely aware of how you are *being* in the process. My wish is for you to embrace joy as a state of well-being with the awareness that joy is a choice, no matter who, what, where, when, or why. When you choose joy, you choose to be who *you* are and who *you* were born to be. By choosing joy, you are choosing YOU. What a privilege.

## Know Yourself

### Scheduling, Spaciousness, Saying NO

By now some of you are probably *more than ready* to begin taking inspired action. Excellent. Remember, the key is not to get hung up on perfect action. Rather, we want to take *inspired* action, rooted in the vision we have for our life, also known as our life purpose.

It may sound obvious, but the reality is that when it comes to taking inspired action, the first step is knowing where we are *today*. As I mentioned in chapter 1, reclaiming joy starts with awareness. With awareness we are able to get really clear and honest about where we are *today*. To give you a structure from which to work, recall from chapter 1 the four foundational areas to well-being: health, relationships, career, life purpose. This is the starting point. Perhaps you relate to some or all of these areas. Maybe you've even added some of your own. Wonderful. Start by getting clear on what your foundational areas are and then where you stand in each. Understanding where we are will help us visualize where we want to go and inspire us to take action.

For example, let's say your heart's desire is to have the freedom to travel whenever you want, yet your current job requires you to be in one place. Starting from where you are today, perhaps you begin visualizing ways to generate income virtually. Whether the job is within your current field of expertise or you're looking for something new, one inspired action from the visualization might be to talk with people – or hire a mentor in your field of interest – who are already successful working virtually. Let's say you choose to initiate a conversation with a person who's already doing what you desire. During the conversation you learn this person is looking for an assistant. Perhaps the assistant is you! The point is, in taking one inspired action fueled by your visualization of where you are *today*, other possibilities will be revealed to you. In the absence of taking inspired action, this opportunity would not have been known to you.

In addition to knowing where we are, the second aspect of taking inspired action is to *know ourselves*. Thankfully, no two people are exactly alike. Since each and every one of us is unique, how we go about living our life is a very individual experience. When we embark on making changes in our life, especially big ones, it may be tempting to play the comparison game. We do this by comparing ourselves to others or to ideas about how we "should" be, based on some idealized version of ourselves. When we do that, we are moving in the opposite direction of reclaiming joy and creating unnecessary suffering.

Why do I say this? Think about it. When we compare ourselves and put the burden of "should" on our shoulders, we place expectations on ourselves that aren't *realistic*. I remember learning this lesson as I began making big changes in my life related to career. When I transitioned from working for someone else in the retail industry to working for myself creating a wellness business, I expected things to happen with the same urgency I had been accustomed to. I quickly discovered that the hard-driving days of multitasking and endless doing were no longer possible for me. Not only was I exhausted from it, I *didn't want* to continue that way of being. This experience became another test for me to put my vision into practice – into action.

It's important to understand that prior to working for myself I valued getting a lot of things done fast. Efficiency and productivity were values that came first, above *all* else. I had to learn how to be in action in a completely new way. I had to slow everything down. Ironically, the "slower way" was one I had previously frowned upon. Now the slower way was becoming the only way I wanted to operate. Imagine that.

It will be no surprise that during this career transition a lot of resistance came up. How did I deal with it? Yes, you guessed it! I engaged in exploring more of my shadows. In the process what was revealed to me was how much of my identity, and therefore confidence, was connected to "getting a lot done." I had to work through many agonizing questions. Who was I if I slowed down and even let a few things slip? What if my website wasn't "perfect"? What if I only wanted to work with a handful of motivated people instead of anyone who showed up at my door? As I worked through these questions, I learned to let go of old ways of being. In doing that, I was making space for new ways to emerge. While it was difficult at times to make changes, my actions were *inspired*. I knew, and still know, that the vision I had for my life was much bigger than my growth spurts. Once again, my life purpose pulled me forward.

As is often the case when we make changes and take inspired action, we learn. Learning is one of the rewards of doing the work. Of course, it wasn't only my career that was in transition. It was me! My whole life, my entire foundation, and everything I had known was falling away, and I was simultaneously being reborn. My authentic self was breaking through the surface. Birth and death. Creation and destruction. The cycle of life. None of us escapes it.

There's a fantastic passage in *The Courage to Create* by Rollo May that talks about what occurs when we have a breakthrough experience.

He says, "*The unconscious seems to take delight in breaking through – and breaking up – exactly what we cling to most rigidly in our conscious thinking. What occurs in this breakthrough is not simply growth; it is much more dynamic. It is not a mere expansion of awareness; it is rather a kind of battle. A dynamic struggle goes on within a person between what he or she consciously thinks on the one hand and, on the other, some insight, some perspective, that is struggling to be born. . . . The guilt that is present when this breakthrough occurs has its source in the fact that the insight must destroy something.... The breakthrough carries with it also an element of anxiety.*"

In this process, as old thoughts and patterns are broken, it shakes our self-world relationship. We have to find new foundations, the forms of which we do not yet know. As this cycle of destruction and creation was unfolding in my life, I paid close attention. By really listening to what supported my well-being based on the four foundational areas, I learned about *who I was becoming*. This wisdom helped me focus my efforts on taking inspired actions that were purposeful and supportive of the vision I had for my life – my desire to reclaim joy by being me. What I also learned during this process was what it would require for me to be successful in staying the course.

To help you start thinking about what *you* may need to be successful, I will share three things I learned about myself during this process, without which I don't feel I would have been successful: First, I must put *myself* on my schedule. Second, I thrive when I have spaciousness in my weekly schedule. Third, the ability to say no is essential. Please allow me to explain.

First, I learned to put *myself* on my schedule. What does this mean? It means that when I plan my week, I block out times for activities that are not related to work. This may be anything from exercising to grocery shopping to meeting up with friends – and anything else that's important to my well-being. To some of you this may sound a bit rigid or even a bit luxurious! Excellent. I understand.

## Reclaiming Joy

When I first start adding myself to my schedule I noticed resistance. Yet what I realized is that if I don't make time for what's important to my well-being, I am simply not living as joy. I am not allowing myself to be me. And my friends, by now joyless living is an old story.

There are also purely practical reasons for adding myself to my schedule. Having non-work-related activities scheduled weekly makes it so much easier to honor my desire for work-life balance. Seeing myself on the schedule solidifies the importance of finding that balance. When I don't schedule time for life outside of work, I begin to feel drained and resentful. Scheduling time for myself also gives me flexibility, so when unexpected things happen, I can see my week and shift things accordingly. By having a schedule that includes what's important to me, it's easier to be relaxed in the uncertainty, stay in the flow, and reprioritize quickly. Putting myself on my schedule creates the space for me to practice ongoing self-care. Perhaps most important is that it reaffirms that *I am worthy* to live the life I want. If I decide to spend three hours doing yoga, that is my choice, and I make it happen. Choice = Freedom = joy!

The second thing I learned about myself is that I thrive when I have *spaciousness* in my weekly schedule. By thrive I mean I have the *energy and desire* to take inspired action. For example, days when I am back-to-back teaching and meeting with clients are not the ideal days for me to engage in creative endeavors such as building workshops and writing a book! Rather, I thrive with creative pursuits when I have an open day and less interaction with people overall. Being aware of this, when I am in creative mode, I include a few days each week when I don't have a set schedule and don't meet with clients. This supports my desire to have a more spacious day.

Including spaciousness in my weekly schedule also creates an environment that supports my energy exchange. For example, on days when I'm interacting with many people (which is a lot of energy output), I may prefer to end my day with a nourishing evening and time alone.

Other times I may want social interaction and to have fun! The point is, it's important to know what nourishes you, recognizing that some days, what usually is nourishing may not be. By managing my energy, I am not as likely to cancel because I've overscheduled myself. I'm aware of my energy and seek to balance the output and input based on what I have going on. Knowing yourself is an ongoing awareness practice. Times when I do have to say no, I will. This leads me to the third thing I learned about myself in order to be successful on this path to reclaiming joy.

The ability to say no is the third thing that is absolutely essential. I have come to believe that when we say no, we are really saying yes! What do I mean? If my intention is to live as joy, the choices I make ought to support that, right? When I say no to someone or something, it's because it *isn't* supporting my desire to live as joy, whatever that means. For example, if after a long day someone is asking me to go to a party, and I am simply not up for it, I will say no. By saying no, I am saying yes to my desire to rest. If I say yes when I mean no, I am self-sabotaging. If I continue to ignore what supports my well-being by saying yes when I mean no, it will catch up with me. My friends, if we continue to ignore our needs over time, we will lose our precious energy and desire to live joyfully.

Perhaps some of you are noticing tension in your body at the thought of saying no. For many people, saying no is a challenge. I have been there, too, and I have survived, even if with a few bruises! Whether we're caught up in the guilt, the "not enough," or the "should" game, to name a few, the practice of learning to say no graciously and without guilt is an art. Furthermore, learning how to say no is *essential* in the process of reclaiming joy. If you doubt it, perhaps this will convince you. I once heard someone say, "I only have two hands and one heart." I take this to mean that in order to help others, we have to know our own limits. Knowing our limits comes as a result of making our well-being and in turn our self-care a priority. In the process we learn how much we are able to handle, and what we need to do in order to nourish ourselves.

# Reclaiming Joy

Remember, we are each unique. Our limits and needs are different and may change over time.

To live as joy, you will have to learn what and how much you are realistically able to do. Your self-care practices will nourish you and help you in saying no. In addition, as you practice saying no, you will free up energy to take inspired actions in the foundational areas important to you. When you say no, not only will you have more energy for yourself, you will have more energy for others. Consider that by saying no in the areas that don't feed your well-being, you will have the energy to start saying yes to the areas that support your well-being. Think *quality* over *quantity*.

Something else to keep in mind about saying no is that at certain times during your life the attention you give to certain foundational areas may shift. For example, if you are in a new relationship, dealing with a sick parent, and work is busier than ever, perhaps you aren't exercising as much as usual. Maybe your health suffers as a result. In addition to practicing compassion for yourself, this is when saying no to what isn't supportive of your well-being becomes even more important. Saying no gives you the necessary freedom to take exquisite care of yourself, no matter what is going on in your life. Remember, the choice is yours. Choose wisely.

Another point I want to clarify is that saying no doesn't mean you only do what you want. Clearly, we all have responsibilities. Rather, what it does mean is that you stay aware of how you are *being* in the *doing*, especially when you are doing the things you view as less than desirable.

Let's take the example of cleaning out the garage, once and for all, in the midst of new relationship, sick parent, busy at work, not exercising "enough." While cleaning out the garage may not be on the top of your joy list, the energy you keep expending thinking about it is draining you. With this awareness you decide to clean out the garage instead of going to spin class then brunch with your friends. Now you have two options of how you will *be* in the *doing*. Will you be miserable or joyful?

Misery will make you tired and miserable. Joy will make you energized and perhaps even grateful.

Does this make sense? You always have a choice about how you are *being* in the *doing*. If the *path* is joy, the *practice* is joy, and the *fruit* is joy. In the doing you choose to be in-joy and en-joy! When you choose to be in-joy and en-joy it, whatever "it" is, this helps solidify your ability to be successful in doing the work to get where you want to go. It also frees you up to accept where *you* are and who *you* are without comparing yourself to others. Finally, it makes your experience of commitment, discipline, accountability, and staying the course an adventurous journey rather than a miserable ride of could have, would have, and should have.

*"Do not be too timid and squeamish about your actions. All life is an experiment. The more experiments you make the better. What if they are a little coarse and you may get your coat soiled or torn? What if you do fail, and get fairly rolled in the dirt once or twice? Up again, you shall never be so afraid of a tumble." —Ralph Waldo Emerson*

### ❋ Reflection Exercise: Know Where You Are

Lovingly rate where you stand in each of your foundational areas using the following scale: 1 = not even close; 5 = in pursuit with struggle; 10 = totally there. In the areas that are 5 and below, take a few minutes to write about what's holding you back. Excuses? Commitment? Lack of clarity or support?

---
---
---
---
---
---
---
---

# Commitment and Discipline

### The 3 Big Excuses: Not Enough Time, Money, Knowledge

On the path to reclaiming joy, taking inspired action requires our deep commitment. As I've mentioned previously, when we fully commit, the universe conspires on our behalf. In addition to receiving support from the universe, we will be shown the areas where we are resisting commitment (our shadows), so that we can work through them. While that work may feel like a curse, it's a gift. As I explained in chapter 2, it's not that we're transforming our darkness into light – we are already light. Instead, we are transforming our perspective, and therefore our thoughts, to support our being.

Having said that, some of you may be wondering, why would we resist committing to a way of being, joy, that seems so wonderful? Well, we are human, remember? It is natural for our human mind to get caught up in the "how." When our mind gets hung up on how, our two friends doubt and fear will reemerge. Don't resist them. They are showing up to help us get closer to being who we are and living the life of our dreams.

The fact is, when we stand in our power and resolve to change ways of being that we have known for so long, as Joseph Campbell said, "We must be willing to give up the life we have planned, so as to have the life that is waiting for us." YES! Our life is waiting for us to stop, look, and listen – to stop driving and start thriving. As we let go of what we think our life "should be," the *excuses* we have made for so long as to why we "can't commit" will reveal themselves. My friends, it is our *excuses* that hold us back from fully committing to the path to reclaiming joy. In the process we are also denying ourselves the privilege of a lifetime – living as joy by being who we are.

In my journey toward reclaiming joy, one of the big excuses I used to make was, "I don't have enough _____" (fill in the blank). Usually the blanks included one of the three precious resources: *time, money, knowledge*. For many of us, not having enough time, money, or knowledge is a powerful excuse – one that's generally accepted and logical to justify.

I promise you that on the path to reclaiming joy, unless our excuses are dealt with directly, honestly, and lovingly, they will derail us. They will create more unnecessary suffering and diminish our ability to commit. Excuses will rob us of joy. So how do we deal with our excuses? Read on.

### Excuse #1 – Not Enough Time

When it comes to commitment, why do we use not having enough *time* as an excuse? In my experience, time is an easy excuse because it is safe. The excuse of not having enough time has become an acceptable justification as to why we aren't living the life we desire. I am here to strongly and lovingly tell you not to buy into it any longer.

I want to share an example. Years ago, when I was offering nutritional coaching, people would often come to me for weight loss. I remember a handful of clients who told me they had *no time* to exercise and that was why they weren't losing weight. It was hard for me to understand not having enough time for something that seemed pretty darn important to them! After some digging, it became clear that they didn't like exercising. In fact, some of them would tell me they hated it. The idea of going to a gym was torture. I understand. I encouraged them to find other ways of movement such as walking outside, dance, even fencing – anything to get their body in motion! I encouraged them to find something they enjoyed, so it wouldn't feel like impossible work. Nothing I suggested worked. Then it hit me. Rather than trying to change their mind by reiterating the benefits of exercise and weight loss (which most of them already knew), I decided to accept this and use a different approach: Enter self-discipline.

On the path to reclaiming joy, there will be things we need to do in pursuit of our larger vision that we don't feel like doing. If someone really wants to lose weight, what they need to exercise is self-discipline. They need to choose some form of movement and do it, whether they like it or not. When I used this approach, it worked for some. They found ways to make exercise more enjoyable and changed their perspective. Those people reframed exercise as something that would *help* them achieve the larger goal of being healthy and having vital energy to enjoy life. Others were simply not ready to commit to improving their health at that time. No judgment. The point in sharing this example is to illustrate that when we admit the truth, *we don't have to hide behind excuses.* Hiding drains our energy. By being honest, we are able to harness our energy and focus on what we are *willing to do* to be successful. In some cases, perhaps the freedom of admitting the truth will refuel our commitment.

The other point this example illustrates about using excuses is the *power of our emotions to derail us* on our path to reclaiming joy. Do you remember from our discussion in chapter 2 that the elephant (our emotions) is far more powerful than and will win the battle against the rider (our mind)? Clearly, our logical mind understands that to lose weight, exercise is important. Yet, as illustrated in the example above, emotions can take over because of a strong dislike of exercise. In this case, *the emotion was so powerful, it created the excuse of time.* What you will continue to learn in this process is that your ability to carry out a commitment depends on your ability to manage your emotions around what you dislike as you practice self-discipline.

As I said, there will be times when we dislike what we have to do, yet we must choose to do it anyway. We choose to do it because we realize it is one step on the journey of a thousand miles – one piece in the bigger picture of our life. As I've said before, our ability to commit tests how much we really want it . . . whatever "it" is. The fact is, if we really want to lose weight, and that is important to us, we will find the time, energy, and inspiration to make it happen. The vision we have for our life, when created from who we are, and what we want, will give us the necessary fuel (energy + desire) to take inspired action, even when we don't feel like it! When we take inspired action, we will be successful.

It's important to reiterate that when we are grounded in awareness and practice self-discipline, we begin to free ourselves from the highly emotional *pain*-and-*pleasure* dance. Meaning, instead of moving back and forth (sometimes multiple times an hour) mentally and emotionally between what we label as pain and pleasure, we remain more in the middle of the two. Living in the middle brings the beginning of the end of this dance that many of us spend decades, or even a lifetime, doing. In the end, we realize this dance does *not* give us peace, freedom, and pleasure. Rather, it gives us trauma, drama, and pain. Writing this reminds me of a favorite passage on "freedom and renunciation" from The Bhagavad Gita: "Unerring in one's discrimination, sovereign of one's senses and passions, free from the clamor of likes and dislikes, one leads a simple, self-reliant life based on meditation, controlling speech, body, and mind". To me this means that when we are rooted in awareness and self-discipline, we free ourselves from the emotional roller coaster. We witness the movie of our life without having to be the star. As we learn how to do that, we also free up precious energy – energy that is waiting to be redirected to living as joy.

Here's one final thought on time. We all have twenty-four hours in a day. My day is different than yours in how I choose to "invest" those hours. I prefer the word invest to *spend*. When I invest, I am making a contribution toward what is important to me. Since I am aware of what supports my well-being based on the four foundational areas, my choices reflect this. If I am making choices that aren't an investment, chances are I will feel drained. My energy leaks because I am not honoring myself, and I will feel there isn't enough time. Upon closer examination, it's not really about having enough time. *My friends, it's about having enough energy!*

Remember I said that health is one of the foundational areas to well-being? In that category I included energy levels. When we are living as joy, by being who we are, we make choices to support that – *choices that enhance our energy rather than drain it.* When we begin to notice the effects of our choices on our energy levels, we no longer allow the constraints of time to be an excuse. Instead, we become more focused and purposeful in how we invest our time based on our desire to live in Ayni (inner alignment). When we live in Ayni, our thoughts, words, and actions are aligned. From this foundation, even when we are doing things we don't love, we have the energy to stay committed to the bigger picture. Finally, since we recognize that we always have a choice about how we are "being" in the "doing," we realize it is far more enjoyable and energizing to be joy. We release not having enough time as an excuse.

## Excuse #2 – Not Enough Money

Not having enough money is the second excuse that often appears when we are faced with commitment on the path to reclaiming joy. What do I mean by not having enough money? In some cases, it's not having enough money in the tangible sense, or at least believing that. I will share more about this later. In other cases, the excuse of not having enough money is connected to a mindset or mentality or general feeling of not *being* enough or worthy. In my experience, this mindset of not *being* enough has a corresponding energetic vibration that influences our behavior and circumstances. This mentality affects all aspects of our life – from how we show up at work to how we show up in our relationships. So while we may be very successful professionally and have plenty of tangible money, we may nevertheless feel that *we* are not enough. This feeling of not *being* enough will eventually show up in other foundational areas of our life, perhaps in relationship, in order to be healed. The story of Nikki that I will share in this section is an example of how a mindset of lack and feelings of not *being* enough can play out in career and relationship and are not necessarily about tangible money.

As you read the pages that follow, keep in mind I am referring to money as a mindset. When we look at our money mindset, it will reveal much about our sense of self and how we view the world around us. If we have been using the excuse of not having enough money as one of the reasons we cannot be successful, this is an opportunity to get clear on what money mindset we are operating from.

In my experience there are two mindsets associated with money that people learn at a very young age. One is lack, and the other is wealth. Each has a corresponding energetic vibration. Lack is low-frequency energy, and wealth is high-frequency energy. These mindsets and frequencies influence our thoughts, words, and actions. They affect how we engage with the world AND how the world engages with *us*. As we become aware of our mindset, and the role it plays in our life, we will stop using lack as an excuse if our desire is to reclaim joy. Let me explain.

Consider the word *lack*. Say it out loud. What do you notice? Maybe nothing. Some of you may notice a feeling of "ick", or you may feel the low frequency this word emits. What other feelings do you notice when you consider the word *lack*? Perhaps anxiety, stress, worry, doubt, fear, contraction? What other words or thoughts come to mind as you say the word? Maybe you are thinking *not enough, not worthy, without, left out, excluded*. Since lack is a mindset, in addition to affecting our thoughts, it affects what we do and don't say (our words), how we feel (our emotions), and ultimately what we do and don't do (our actions). Pretty powerful, wouldn't you agree?

To illustrate how a lack mentality can impact our life, let's look at a client experience I had with a woman I'll call Nikki. Nikki came to me for a shamanic energy healing session with the desire to attract into her life a long-term intimate relationship. She felt something was getting in the way of her manifesting this and was ready for it to be released. Then in her late forties, she had spent most of her adult life working hard at being successful in business. She felt accomplished in the foundational area of career and was ready for a committed relationship. When I asked her what she felt was getting in the way, she said it was *difficult for her to ask for what she wanted* when it came to intimate or close relationships. Since she was a success in her field, clearly she was able to use her voice in certain situations. However, when it came to matters of her heart, she was blocked.

What our session revealed was that at a very young age, Nikki repeatedly got the message that she was not enough, not worthy of asking for and receiving what she wanted. She recounted many painful instances when she was told no by her parents for no apparent reason. Over time, she began to believe she wasn't worthy of asking. She made an agreement with herself that it was better for her *not* to ask, because if she did, she would be rejected. Especially as a child, feeling rejected by our parents is painful, scary, and unsafe. In order to feel safe, Nikki quickly learned that as long as she didn't ask, she wouldn't have to deal with the "pain of being rejected." She simply stopped asking. She denied herself her voice, and, thus, her needs remained unmet.

As an adult, when it came to intimate relationships, Nikki was unable to speak from her heart to ask for what she wanted. She was still operating from the lack/not enough/not worthy mentality, rooted in fear of rejection. The thought of asking for her needs to be met from an intimate partner created such anxiety, stress, and contraction in her body that she didn't dare do it. She was literally terrified. She channeled this unworthy energy into creating a successful career. Nikki wasn't *consciously* aware of operating from lack. Due to the success she experienced in her career, she felt accomplished, at least materially. Because she was financially successful, it didn't occur to her that she was operating from a lack mentality in her intimate relationships. Clearly, her career success gave her some sense of worth, yet it wasn't the kind her heart was longing for. Deep within her subconscious, there was a need to heal the not worthy/not enough wound. It was the area of intimate relationship, as is often the case, that brought these deep wounds to light.

By the end of our session, after clearing this energy block, Nikki was able to see how the lack mentality and low-frequency energy kept her contracted and unable to meet someone. Her desire to have an intimate relationship was so strong at this stage of her life that she was willing to commit and take inspired action to shift from the lack mentality to the wealth mentality.

I want to point out something else in this example that relates to the shadow work discussed in chapter 2. Recall that our shadows are the parts of ourselves we disown or deny. Yet they are also the places of our greatest gifts. In order to deal with the no responses she heard as a child, Nikki stopped asking. She stifled her voice to protect her heart from feeling rejected by her parents. *As a result of masking one part of herself in order to feel safe (stifling her voice), she raised the volume on another part by doing well in school and ultimately creating a successful career (the gifts*). Essentially, the effect of masking one area brings greater attention to another. Nikki's actions were fueled by her lack mentality, albeit unconsciously, and she ended up becoming very good in another area of life – in this case, career. By channeling energy into her career, she was attempting to feel that she was enough, worthy, in order to feel accepted and safe in at least one foundational area of her life. Since feeling safe is fundamental to our well-being, when we don't feel safe as children, as adults it will show up in order for us to heal. In Nikki's case, as an adult she didn't feel safe speaking her voice and asking for her needs to be met because she felt unheard and unworthy as a child. When she asked, she heard no. The unworthy was channeled in a positive way in her career, and she met with success. However, in her intimate relationships, the unworthy energy made it impossible for her to ask for what she needed, and therefore she didn't have success in relationships. This aspect of unworthy came up in relationship to be healed. Since the universe wants us to heal, whatever we need to heal will eventually show up in one of the four foundational areas: health, relationship, career, life purpose. Yes, the universe at work again!

As I've mentioned previously, with all shadow work, there are gifts in these dark experiences. Being able to see the gifts gives meaning to our journey to reclaiming joy, and we experience healing, empowerment, and, ultimately, freedom. By seeing our negative experiences as opportunities for healing and growth, we are free to be who we are, right NOW. We realize we don't have to wait until we fix or have the right childhood/body/job/relationship/spiritual practice. Instead, we learn how to turn our wounds into sources of power and compassion, giving us even more fuel for the journey.

Based on Nikki's career success, she clearly has the skills to make commitments and take inspired action. Her growth now is in learning how to nourish and love herself because of who she is at this exact moment. This self-love will provide her with the nectar to take actions in her life that help her feel worthy. As she does that, she will begin to ask for what she wants, recognizing that doing so is an act of self-love. Over time she will realize that no job or relationship, nothing or no one – not even her parents' love and acceptance – is required to make her worthy. She has always been worthy and always will be. *My dear friends, this is the shift from the lack mentality to the wealth mentality.*

Now let's take a look at *wealth*. Say the word *wealth* out loud. Notice what happens in your body. Are you excitedly shouting "Yes!" and feeling a sense of energy run through you? Or are you noticing contraction and a sense of tightness in your body? Try not to judge what comes up; simply observe. Your reaction is part of understanding your personal relationship and mindset with money. If you have a wealth mindset, your thoughts likely include words such as worthy, more than enough, plenty. Your associated feelings may be those of gratitude, ease, and expansion.

Let's stay with our Nikki example as we explore the effects of shifting from a lack mentality to a wealth one. Nikki's strong desire to attract an intimate relationship gave her the necessary fuel to embrace a wealth mentality and take inspired actions. Part of her inspired actions include exploring ways to deeply nourish herself on a regular basis. Perhaps she will discover the importance of setting boundaries at work by saying no more often when asked to stay late. Other ways to nourish herself may include taking exquisite care of her physical body with massage, healthy food, and adequate rest. On the spiritual side, she may want to develop a daily ritual of meditation to help her deepen her awareness and connect to her inner wisdom.

As Nikki takes actions to nourish herself, she is sending an important message to her physical, mental, and emotional body: I am worthy and I am enough. She *deserves* to feel good. By making self-love a priority, and engaging in nourishing activities on a consistent basis, she will become accustomed to how doing so makes her feel – expansive, loved, worthy. These feel-good emotions will feed her and keep her at it, so to speak. With practice, she will accept nothing less. Why would she?

My friends, when we make choices and engage in activities that support our well-being, we feel empowered to ask for what we need from others. The practice of self-love starts with *us*. It starts with having generosity toward ourselves – first. Until we are generous to and with ourselves, it will be hard for others to do it for us.

Perhaps more important is that from an energetic perspective, *we attract who we are*. If we are operating from lack, we attract people and situations that "take" from us. It's that place of contraction, remember? Why does this happen? Because we allow it! On the other hand, when we shift to a wealth mentality, we begin to attract people and circumstances that give to us. We feel expansive, grateful and are open to possibilities.

When Nikki begins to ask for what she wants, even when she's told no, she won't experience emotional collapse. She may get triggered and not like it, but because she is aware and nourished by self-love, she will bounce back and have the clarity to do what is required. In some cases, as she begins to stand in her power and ask for what she wants, people will begin to respect her strength and courage. More and more she will attract people into her life who resonate with her energetic vibration of wealth. As this happens, more and more opportunities will reveal themselves in *all* areas of her life. The synergistic effect of this will keep her courage muscle growing. When she finds herself in the tender space of heart, in intimate relationships, she will be able to ask for what she wants and believe she is worthy of receiving. She will accept nothing less than what supports her well-being. This is true wealth.

Some of you may be thinking, yes, this sounds great, but I literally don't have the tangible money for "_____" (fill in the blank). I hear you. This is where understanding the power of your thoughts and words to create your reality is even more essential. If you believe not having enough tangible money is the reason you are unable to commit and therefore aren't able to be successful, then that is what will play out. Remember earlier when I spoke of visualization? I shared that when we visualize, without worrying about "how," we open to possibility. In that space, fear, doubt, and worry aren't present. Think about it. Attaching to "how" is simply another form of control that is rooted in lack. I would even go so far as to say that when we obsess about how, we are making another excuse. More on this later! The point is, when we are in *lack*, we are in a place of not trusting that we will get what we need, in both our unconscious and our conscious mind. As a result, our thoughts and our words are negative, and we send out this low energy to the universe. What do you think we will receive in return? You guessed it. Affirmation of what we are focusing on: that we will *not* get what we need. The trick in living from the wealth mindset is to *visualize* exactly what it is you desire and to *act as if* you are already receiving it. You must have faith. You must prepare yourself to receive. If you don't believe it, the universe *will* know.

For example, let's say you are in need of five thousand dollars to invest in working with a mentor to help you create a profitable and purpose-driven business. In order to attract this money into your life, you spend time every day visualizing the money coming to you. Perhaps you *see* heaps of cash at your doorstep. You *smell* money, and you *hear* the crumple of the fresh bills under your feet as you reach down to pick them up. You connect emotionally to what it *feels* like to receive five thousand dollars so effortlessly – love, expansion, gratitude, confidence, and empowerment. The high vibration of these emotions will attract exactly what you desire. Furthermore, when you *act as if*, you practice saying thank you in advance of receiving. The universe appreciates gratitude. Actually, it seems gratitude is the preferred currency of the universe. Invest in gratitude and express it often in thought, word, and action. Your life will change dramatically.

In her book *The Game of Life and How to Play It*, Florence Scovel Shinn does a fantastic job of elaborating on acting as if, preparing to receive, and the power of our thoughts and words in getting what we want. To illustrate, here are a few of my favorite lines from her book:

> On acting as if when attracting money: "*Order an expensive luncheon, act as if you have already received the three thousand dollars.*"

On preparing to receive: *"Man must prepare for the thing he has asked for, when there isn't the slightest sign of it in sight. Man can only receive what he sees himself receiving."*

On the power of our words: *"Thus the invisible forces are ever working for man, who is always 'pulling the strings' himself, though he does not know it. Owing to the vibratory power of words, whatever man voices, he begins to attract."*

Are you convinced yet, my faithful friends? Truly, you will change your circumstances and be able to reclaim joy, however that looks for you, by changing your thoughts and thereby your words. It starts with awareness. Awareness enables you to make *conscious* choices. When we make conscious choices, we are supporting ourselves in reclaiming joy. As we reclaim joy, we are living into the vision we have for our own unique life. Because the vision we have for our life is who we are fundamentally, we are energized to receive, and we have the necessary fuel to take inspired actions. When we face challenges, our deep commitment supports us in exercising the necessary self-discipline to stay on the path. With practice, living as joy, being who we are, becomes the *only* way. Any other way of being is simply *not* an option. YES!

By now you may be feeling rather full with all of this money talk. Exhale. Money is a big topic for most of us, and it brings up all kinds of emotions. Practice BRFWA. Ride the emotional wave. Let it go. As I said earlier, my intention for bringing up the topic of money is to show how at times we use it as an excuse for why we don't have what we want or why we "can't" have what we want. In reality, money isn't the issue. *The issue is our mindset and the corresponding energetic vibration we are sending out.* If money is a hot spot for you, continue exploring it and consider reading Florence Scovel Shinn's book mentioned above. Understanding how we relate to money is an eye-opening process that is essential for staying committed on the path to reclaiming joy.

### Excuse #3 – Not Enough Knowledge

The third excuse we often use when it comes to being unable to commit is not having enough *knowledge*. When you think of the word *knowledge*, what comes to mind? If you are like me, maybe you think of the world of the "seen" – tangible stuff like facts and figures that can be proved or measured in some way. What about the word *wisdom*? Maybe you think of the world of the "unseen" – intuition, the little voice, a deep inner knowing that is not able to be proved, only felt.

Why am I asking this? For many of us, knowledge is the third big excuse we make when we don't commit to going after what we desire. We tell ourselves we don't know enough or know how. There it is again! The doubt and worry. The fact is, we will never know enough. And guess what? That isn't such a bad thing. In my experience, it is when we think we know it all, that we close ourselves off to possibility. If you recall, possibility is what keeps us in the flow of receiving through the practice of visualizing. When we stop living in possibility, we also dampen our creativity. Often it's when we are in the process of creating that we are most resourceful and receive so much more than our limited mind tells us.

No doubt some of you have heard the phrase "beginner's mind", a concept from Buddhism. Beginner's mind means we are free of preconceived notions, open, and eager to learn. When we practice beginner's mind, we are willing to accept that we don't know it all, and we allow life to unfold. Perhaps we become ever more curious as we begin to train ourselves to see with new eyes. We see opportunities that weren't there before. They were, though! We simply weren't *trained* to see them.

On the path to reclaiming joy, understanding the difference between wisdom and knowledge is crucial. When we have that understanding, we will know the difference between truly lacking commitment and simply making an excuse. Truly lacking commitment may mean that our inner wisdom is trying to tell us to adjust our path in some way. Perhaps an old pattern is surfacing, and we're forcing ourselves in a direction based on "should." As we connect to our inner wisdom, we need to ask ourselves *why* we are unable to commit. If we stay open and have faith, we will gain clarity on our next steps.

On the other hand, if we are not committing with the excuse of not knowing enough or how, perhaps it's an invitation for us to work on our self-discipline. As a human being, chances are there will be certain times in your life when you have more discipline than others. That's normal. Accept it and if you don't have the discipline you need, get support, either by hiring a mentor or by enlisting someone to hold you accountable. The fact is, whatever the reason for the lack of commitment, so be it. The key is to bring it into the light of your awareness. When you do, you will be able to make the appropriate choice to keep you on track and taking inspired actions. Don't waste your precious life making excuses!

### ❋ Reflection Exercise: What's My Excuse?

Take a few minutes to write about the following questions:

What excuses are standing in the way of your commitment to reclaiming joy? What is one inspired action you will take based on your findings?

_____
_____
_____
_____
_____
_____
_____
_____
_____
_____
_____
_____
_____
_____

# Sweet Surrender

### En-joy and In-joy

At this point I have spoken at length about the importance of awareness in reclaiming joy. In the last three chapters I have invited you to consider many things, such as what supports your well-being by looking at the four foundational areas and what gets you stuck. We have looked at how to gain meaning from our experiences and use the learning as fuel for our growth. At the same time, we have discussed what is required to take inspired action in support of the vision we have for our life. I have encouraged you to take an honest look at excuses that may arise and have stressed the importance of commitment and self-discipline. We have covered quite a bit of material! Let's exhale and give thanks for *all* of it. Now it's time to look at the last key ingredient in reclaiming joy.

After all is said and done, the key to living as joy (en-joy and in-joy) is surrender. I realize the word *surrender* may have different meanings for each of us, so allow me to clarify. *Quite simply, surrender means not being attached to the results of our actions.* It means *letting go.* Some of you might be thinking this makes no sense. Why would we not be attached to results if ultimately it's for our well-being? Isn't that the whole point? Yes and no.

Yes, you have taken the time to do so much already simply by reading this book! You've deepened your awareness about what supports your well-being; you have met and perhaps even worked with some of your shadows; you may have started visualizing your life; some of you have already taken inspired actions; others of you have seriously committed and are already noticing your joy returning. Bravo to all, wherever you find yourself. Having put forth this effort, *why must you now surrender?* What is the reasoning behind releasing all attachment to the results you so very much want?

The fact is, in the long run, the practice of surrender is the only way to truly reclaim joy. There are two reasons for this. First, when we surrender, we allow something much bigger than ourselves to carry us forward. Second, when we surrender, we accept that we are not in control.

I've spoken at length about the power of visualization and that to be successful we must release ourselves from the burden of worrying about "how" something will happen. When we release "how," we're engaging in a form of surrender by practicing nonattachment. By not attaching to how something will happen, we allow our imagination to run wild and open ourselves up to ever more possibilities. On the other hand, when we are attached to "how," we limit ourselves to only what our doubting mind is showing us. By surrendering to the how, we expand our imagination and begin to see possibilities that our mind simply wasn't able to come up with. In *The Game of Life and How to Play It*, Florence Scovel Shinn says, *"Demonstrations often come at the eleventh hour because man then let's go, that is, stops reasoning, and Infinite Intelligence has a chance to work."* In essence what she is saying is that once we get out of the way and let go by means of surrender to a power greater than ourselves, the universe has a chance to conspire on our behalf. As I have mentioned several times, the universe has our best interests at hand.

An example of this from my own life happened the summer of 2014 when I was thinking about taking a six-month sabbatical in honor of my fortieth birthday the following year. My doubting mind gave me all the reasons it was not possible and too extravagant. After all, I own a wellness sanctuary and in addition to working with clients, teaching classes, and running workshops, I am heavily involved in the business side of running the sanctuary. Yet I was determined to explore the possibility.

Over the summer I used my daily meditation practice to visualize my sabbatical happening and to ask for guidance. At the end the summer an opportunity presented itself to attend a three-week yoga leadership training in Bali the following spring. At the time I was interested in deepening my yoga leadership training. After I looked into the program I knew this opportunity was a sign. I decided to plan my six-month sabbatical around the training in Bali. In the planning, everything I needed came effortlessly. I found people to sub my classes, and there was an ease in creating spaciousness in my schedule. In the end I wound up taking off the first six months of 2015. I spent five weeks in Bali to participate in the training and to travel. In addition to Bali I attended a few other trainings in the U.S. and enjoyed having time off to play, explore, and have nothing to do.

My sabbatical was blissful and life changing. It would not have happened if I had been attached to how it could happen. By releasing how and surrendering, the opportunities presented themselves without me having to do anything except *pay attention.* Awareness! I had not "planned" to go to Bali. I wasn't even looking for it! I was simply visualizing my sabbatical while asking for guidance and to be shown something. I was patient and had faith that whatever I was supposed to be doing would reveal itself. Whenever my mind tried to engage me in doubt, which it did, especially when I shared my idea with other well-meaning humanoids, I practiced surrender. Had I allowed myself to get caught up in doubt, my own or others', I would have missed out on an incredible experience. My entire sabbatical experience gave me the opportunity to slow down even more and to enjoy a spaciousness I craved and needed.

As I mentioned previously, spaciousness in my schedule is important, and I design my life to support that. When I have spaciousness, I am creative and gain clarity. My sabbatical fueled my creative fire and showed me other possibilities in terms of my career, one of which is writing this book! I also gained insight into my personal life and recognized opportunities for growth in my intimate relationships. There were countless other gifts I received from taking time off – from making new friends to discovering how much cooking for others nourishes me. In the end, what I want you to take away from this example is that *when we surrender, we allow something larger than ourselves to move us forward* and show us the way. On the path to reclaiming joy, surrendering to something larger than ourselves keeps us open and frees up our energy so that we may receive what is already waiting for us. You see, we really don't have to work that hard. We really can stop driving and start thriving. We simply need to have enough faith to surrender and then pay attention.

This brings me to the second reason we need to surrender if our desire is to reclaim joy. When we surrender, we *accept* that we are *not* in control. Some of you might be exploring control as part of your shadow work. For me it has been and continues to be something I am aware of as a challenge within myself. When we think we are in control, we feel safe. Yet as we know, control gives us a false sense of safety. The reality is, no matter how much we plan and protect, things happen unexpectedly, and often it's what we didn't even consider. If you are like me, at some point you realize how much of your precious energy is wasted in trying to control outcomes. And at some point, you are willing to consider letting that go. Let's face it, trying to be in control is not only exhausting, it isn't very much fun. Holding on to being in control keeps us from experiencing joy because it works in direct opposition to what reclaiming joy is all about.

Instead of putting energy into trying to control, what if we simply take inspired action and then let go? By surrendering to the reality that we are not in control, we take action and practice nonattachment to results. By practicing nonattachment to results, we accept what happens. It doesn't mean we don't care about what happens. Of course we care! However, when we actively practice surrender, we release expectations and allow divine intelligence to take over. By allowing divine intelligence to take over, we stay open to infinite possibilities. We realize that perhaps the result our mind is telling us we desire is not what is in our best interest. In addition, we show the universe we are trusting and grateful. Remember, the universe thrives on trust and gratitude. I have another example of this, but before I give it, another quote awaits. This is from *The Bhagavad Gita*, on self-realization:

"You have the right to work, but never to the fruit of work. You should never engage in action for the sake of reward, nor should you long for inaction. Perform work in this world . . . without selfish attachments, and alike in success and defeat."

When I read this quote, it fills me with a sense of ease. The practice of nonattachment, the place of an even, steady mind, liberates me to be myself without the pressure of having to perform. And it's so much more FUN. Okay, back to the example I want to share that illustrates the power of nonattachment.

When I transitioned from my corporate career to my wellness business, I started teaching in adult education centers. I really wanted to put myself out there, so I contacted every adult education center possible. As a result, I was busy running around teaching. In some centers I had great success with full classes and engaged students. In other centers class was a flop, or in some cases the class was cancelled due to low interest. When this happened, naturally I would get upset. I would waste energy and at times got discouraged. Over time I realized that unless I practiced surrendering to the results and showed up without expectations, I would continually be on this roller coaster of emotions.

So I practiced surrendering to outcome. The result? I had more energy. Instead of worrying about outcomes, I channeled my energy to develop the discipline to show up with gratitude and openness. My focus became to simply share what I love in service to whoever was there I was meant to help. As I practiced surrendering to outcomes and results, the better results I got. I felt more present with my students. I was fun, more engaging, and better able to adjust my presentation to who showed up that evening. In the end, I had far fewer flops, and we all experienced much more fun. The message was clear. I am not entitled to the fruit of my actions. I am there to serve, and I need to let go of the rest. It was a freeing and humbling lesson. Over time, by showing up without attachment, I had the presence of mind to see which centers were a good fit for me. Since then I have added the practice of surrender to everything I do. Easy? Not always. Worth it? Yes! In order for me to be myself and live as joy, the practice of surrender is essential.

The thing that has taught me the most about surrender is meditation.

Surrendering is a felt sense that is best understood by experiencing it rather than using words. However, since this is a book, here is how surrender feels to me. This is taken from *The Bhagavad Gita:*

"When meditation is mastered, the mind is unwavering like the flame of a lamp in a windless place. In the still mind, in the depths of meditation, the Self reveals itself. Beholding the Self by means of the Self, an aspirant knows the joy and peace of complete fulfillment. Having attained that abiding joy beyond the senses, revealed in the stilled mind, he never swerves from the eternal truth. He desires nothing else, and cannot be shaken by the heaviest burden of sorrow."

As I said at the start of this book, reclaiming joy starts with awareness. For me, meditation is the awareness practice that blew open everything else. Meditation has brought me to where I am today and has enabled me to practice surrender. Like awareness, surrender is an ongoing practice. As you go about your journey, remember the practice of surrender is the only way to truly reclaim joy, to be who you are. What will you choose?

As I have said many times before, joy is a state of being. That said, if I am doing what makes me happy yet am still caught in the worry of results, I am not being joy. Rather I am being fearful, controlling, and doubtful. The process of reclaiming joy in my own life has taught me that in order to be myself and live as joy, no matter what is going on, *I have a choice.* So even when I am doing what I love – and practicing nonattachment to results – and for whatever reason I am not connecting to my students, or something doesn't turn out as I "thought" I wanted, I choose joy. I choose to be in-joy and to en-joy the experience, no matter what.

That is the golden nugget of everything I have written in these pages. *The secret to reclaiming joy is to be in-joy and to en-joy all of it.* Perhaps Joyce Brothers said it best: "When it comes right down to it, the secret of having it all is loving it all." Yes! For me, having it all means being joy. It means being who I am, which is love and light. Being joy is *not* based on what I am doing or not doing, or what I am getting or not getting.

# Reclaiming Joy

Being joy is about loving all of what is here. Loving the beauty and the beast the same. For me, loving all of what is here is possible only when I am free to be who I am. The freedom to be me is what my journey to reclaiming joy has been about. It is the journey I took to stop driving and start thriving . . . a journey that has given me the gifts of happiness, health, and freedom.

## ✳ Reflection Exercise: Experiment in Surrender

Take a few moments to reflect on what *surrender* means to you. Where or how in your life can you start to practice surrender? Write down what comes to mind and consider practicing surrender in that area for the next thirty days. At the end of thirty days, come back to what you wrote. Reflect on what you noticed about your experience. Decide what's next. More practice in this same area? Perhaps you are ready to move on to another area? Choose and repeat the process as often as needed.

## Chapter Summary and Reflection

In this chapter I spoke about how we actually start to live as joy. Specifically, I shared the value of knowing yourself in terms of what you need to feel nourished so you have the necessary energy and desire to choose joy as a way of being. I also discussed the three big excuses that often prevent us from fully committing: not having enough time, not having enough money, not having enough knowledge. I talked about the importance of cultivating discipline to support you on your journey. Finally, I spoke about how surrender is the secret ingredient to living as joy.

My hope is that this book has given you some of the tools to begin living as joy, by *being who you are*. As you courageously embark on the journey to reclaiming joy, remember to be in-joy as you en-joy. I joyously support you.

*"The highest form of spiritual practice is non-judgmental compassionate self-awareness."*
—Swami Kripalu

# Resources

I've provided here the beginning of each quotation in the book, followed by its source.

## Introduction

"The privilege of. . ." Diane K. Osbon. *Reflections on the Art of Living: A Joseph Campbell Companion*. HarperCollins: New York, 1991, p. 15.

## Chapter One

"As a person fluctuates. . ." Steven R. Covey. *The 7 Habits of Highly Effective People*. Free Press: New York, 1989, p. 122.

"By centering our lives. . ." Ibid., p.123.

"Will this choice. . ." Debbie Ford. *The Right Questions: Ten Essential Questions to Guide You to an Extraordinary Life*. HarperCollins: New York, 2004, p. 7.

"When you no longer. . . " Geneen Roth. *Women, Food and God*. Scribner: New York, 2010, p. 80-81.

"In fact the American. . . " Nina Radcliff. *Chronic stress: The silent killer if not managed*. http://www.washingtontimes.com/news/2015/jan/6/nina-radcliff-chronic-stress-silent-killer-if-not-/

"It is the creation. . . " Daphne Rose Kingma. *Coming Apart: Why Relationships End and How to Live through the Ending of Yours.* Conari Press: California, 2000, p. 29.

"We work first. . . " Stephen Cope. *The Great Work of Your Life: A Guide for the Journey to Your True Calling.* Bantam Books: New York, 2012, p. 249.

## Chapter Two

"When a person. . . " Paulo Coelho. *The Alchemist—25$^{th}$ Anniversary Edition.* HarperCollins: New York, 1993, p. 118.

"The common belief. . . " David R. Hawkins, M.D., Ph.D. *Power vs. Force: An Anatomy of Consciousness.* Veritas: Arizona, 2004, p. 84.

"The voice induced. . . " Geneen Roth. *Women, Food and God.* Scribner: New York, 2010, p. 141.

"The unspeakable cruelty. . . " Jalaja Bonheim. *Aphrodite's Daughters: Women's Sexual Stories and the Journey of the Soul.* Fireside: New York, 1997, p. 240.

## Chapter Three

"Our deepest fear. . . " Marianne Williamson. *A Return to Love: Reflections on the Principles of "A Course in Miracles."* HarperCollins: New York, 1992, p. 190-191.

## Chapter Four

"The unconscious seems. . . " Rollo May. *The Courage to Create.* W.W. Norton: New York, 1975, p. 59-60.

"Do not be. . . " Ralph Waldo Emerson. *http://www.goodreads.com/quotes/375347-do-not-be-too-timid-and-squeamish-about-your-actions*

"Unerring in discrimination. . . " Eknath Easwaran, ed. *The Bhagavad Gita.* Nilgiri Press: Canada, 2007, p. 262.

"Order an expensive. . . " Florence Scovel Shinn. *The Collection: "The Game of Life and How to Play It."* Tribeca Books: USA, 2015, p. 6.

"Man must prepare. . . " Ibid., p. 7.

"Thus the invisible. . . " Ibid., p. 11.

"Demonstrations often come. . . " Ibid., p. 47.

"You have the right. . . " Eknath Easwaran, ed. *The Bhagavad Gita.* Nilgiri Press: Canada, 2007, p. 94.

"When meditation is. . . " Ibid., p. 142.

# Speaker Highlight

*Interested in having Stephanie speak at your next event?*

## Topics include:

Thriving You: 4 Foundations of Well-Being

Healthy You: Food and Mood Connection

Relaxed You: Meditation and Stress Management

Joyful You: Conscious Communication and Relationships

Spirited You: Spiritual Practice and Life Purpose

Wealthy You: Purpose Driven and Profitable Business

For more information contact:

stephanie@thrivingyouthrivinglife.com

or visit www.thrivingyouthrivinglife.com

32412839R00066

Made in the USA
Middletown, DE
03 June 2016